THE
COMMANDMENTS
AND THE
NEW MORALITY

Nicholas Lohkamp, O.F.M.

with Leonard Foley, O.F.M.

Nihil Obstat:
    Rev. Hilarion Kistner, O.F.M.
    Rev. John J. Jennings

Imprimi Potest:
    Rev. Roger Huser, O.F.M.
    Provincial

Imprimatur:
    ✝Joseph L. Bernardin
    Archbishop of Cincinnati
    November 6, 1973

Illustration and design
by Michael Reynolds

SBN 0-912228-11-3

Contents

Chapter I

CHANGE OF FOCUS:

Persons Come into Their Own

the gray ABC camera peers down impartially from the rim of the stadium and slowly swings from left to right, a stiffnecked robot recording the presence of 100,000 Rose Bowl fans. On millions of TV sets there is a rectangle of 100,000 dots, indistinguishable as persons. Just dots. Spectators all. Football fans. That's *what* you see.

The right side of the stadium is Southern Cal's. Fifty thousand rooters. All the same? The camera can't say. Fifty-thousand dots. That's *what* you see.

By the magic of a zoom lens, the 50,000 dots suddenly flow forward on the screen, and we get a close-up of one face — a middle-aged man solemnly eating a hot dog.

Now, if you said anything about the picture, it wouldn't be, *"What* is that?" — unless the hot dog was lavender, or there was a large bug on the man's head. You might say, "I wonder *who* he is? Why are

1

they concentrating on *him? Who's he?*"

He's a *who,* mainly, and only secondarily a *what.* And in that apparently silly play of words we have the basis for examining one of the recent changes in moral theology: the shift in emphasis from nature to person.

What We Are — Our Nature

The man on the screen is indeed a *what.* If you really said "What is that?", the only answer would be "It's a human being, a body-spirit unity, with freedom and intelligence, feelings and sensations."

That's what he is. That's his nature. And you can say that again — about three billion times — about every human being on earth. We are talking about nature, human nature.

We have all kinds of data about *it.* We believe that certain things are good for it, and good to be done; other things harmful to it, and bad to do. If we saw him slip his hand into the next person's pocket and extricate a wallet, we would judge, "That's bad." If he smiles at the girl next to him, "That's good."

So far, all we have is "whats." They are helpful in talking about some general obligations and rights this man has — they do enter into a discussion of the commandments whereby this man comes to God, but they are not enough.

Who is this man?

Now you're talking about a person, and whatever you say now, you cannot say again about anyone else on earth, at least in the same way.

He's Harry Shoemaker, and he's not from California and he's not rooting for Southern Cal, even if he's on their side. He's in Pasadena because his kid brother has been arrested for stealing a car. He doesn't like hot dogs, but hasn't had the opportunity to eat lunch until now. He bought a ticket for the game from a scalper at the last moment, just to have something to do while he waited to go back home. His trip had been futile.

Harry's from Detroit, where he works on the assembly line at Ford. Newspaper labels would call him a "middle-class ethnic," a hardhat. Labels again. "Whats." The men at the factory call him "Hank" and when they say "Hank" they have just one unique individual in mind. He's the only guy in the world who's married to Helen Evans. Nobody else in the world is the father of Bill, Wanda and Joey Shoemaker. Half a million men fought in Vietnam, but no other soldier could sit in the jungle and remember the time *his* father and mother gave him that bicycle for Christmas. Nobody else in the stadium ever had a fifth grade teacher tell him that *his* drawing of Lincoln was silly.

Nobody else in the world is good or bad, moral or immoral, exactly the way Harry Shoemaker is. If he prays, steals, reads to his kids or curses a foreman, there is no human action in the world that is good or bad precisely the way his is.

The camera turns from Harry, and again we have 100,000 dots. From one "who" to many "whats." As "whats" they're all the same. As "whos" each one is as unique as Harry Shoemaker.

To state the shift in moral theology in a very simple way, then, one could say that no one loves or

3

sins, is guilty or admirable as a "dot," as *merely* someone with "human nature." We are what we are, each of us, because human nature has been "put into" three billion distinct and unique persons in the world today.

"Man" doesn't love or hate. Only Harry Shoemaker does.

What occurred, then, especially in the last 75 years, is a gradual shift of *emphasis* and *focus.* Studies in philosophy and theology, especially Scripture, and advances in psychology, anthropology and sociology have stimulated this change of *focus* in morality. It is not a choice between nature *or* person. It is a question of primary focus. The aspect of "nature" (source of human activity) continues to be present and important. But, once the focus shifts to the human "person" (the one who actually expresses himself in activity), some very important changes in moral considerations occur. "Nature" is no longer seen as the main aspect: the primary focus is the person.

There is no doubt that some of Harry's behavior has basic moral meaning because it agrees with or contradicts his *nature* as a human being. It makes a big difference whether he takes care of his kids or continually neglects and abuses them. Traditional morality has always stressed this "out there" *(objective)* aspect of human behavior. Trouble arose, however, to the extent that the main emphasis was placed on the behavior itself, in the light of human *nature.*

There was a great tendency to categorize some human behavior as "contrary to nature and therefore evil," without considering what might be going on *inside* the individual *person*. There was a corresponding tendency to *assume* that anyone who behaved in that way was guilty of sin.

What would you have judged about Harry Shoemaker? Is he a Southern Cal rooter? A football fan? What's his attitude to the girl he smiled at? Did he really steal that wallet?

Consider some examples. Joe No. 1 grew up in a slum, knowing almost nothing of parental love, acceptance, hope or responsibility. He learned a lot about fear, hate, a dog-eat-dog philosophy, self-defense, anger and violence. Now he steals whatever and whenever he can — car batteries, tires, purses, unguarded merchandise, his mother's grocery money.

Joe No. 2 is the ideal American. Good education, nice family, a home in the suburbs, vice-presidency at Soap, Inc. He is highly regarded by friends and associates. Yet he cuts corners morally, makes payoffs, deceives buyers to increase his profits.

Joe No. 3 is a hard-working honest man not too far above the poverty level. Wants his kids to have a good education, goes to church, works hard. He finds himself overwhelmed with bills and is in danger of losing his home. He has a chance to steal or embezzle enough money to tide him over, and he takes it, intending to pay it back when he can.

In all these examples there is question of stealing and deceit. Seen from the focus of "nature," they are the same; and they are all wrong. But it is evident that while in all three cases the activity (stealing and deceit) is of the same kind, we cannot morally evaluate such activity in any real or full sense without focusing on the *person* involved.

The Shift to Emphasis on Person

How can we describe a moral outlook that puts an increased emphasis on *person?* Keeping Harry Shoemaker and the three Joes in mind, we can say the following:

1) *Personal* Morality must go beyond statements about the "nature" of man (all very necessary) to considerations of man's full personal reality. How does Joe No. 1's personal history affect his moral awareness now? Is there anything else involved in Joe No. 2's personal moral dossier besides all the "good" facts? Does the desperation that Joe No. 3 personally experiences reduce his guilt?

In other words, the human person is a *unity,* and moral responsibility is to be judged in the light of personal unity and continuity. The bodily and spiritual aspects, the knowledge and freedom, the emotions and feelings, the hopes and desires, dreams and goals, as well as the circumstances in which he finds himself — *all* of these have a basic bearing on the moral significance of *this* person's behavior.

2) Another important aspect of a morality that emphasizes the personal is the matter of *relationship.* No man is an island. No one will be saved or damned as an isolated individual. To be a person is to be in relationship with others. God made man to become a person by receiving others' love and responding in love. If a baby were totally isolated

from human contacts, he would die. He will "die" as a person if he does not continue those relationships into adult life. The Two Great Commandments — and the Ten — all have to do with relationships to God and to fellow men.

3) A third aspect of person-centered morality has to do with the fact that we are *the bearers of our own past*. There are no isolated actions; the morality of an action does not come "out of the blue," suddenly, divorced from the momentum of the moment before, the day before, the year before. To evaluate anyone's actions morally we must know his habits and attitudes (which cannot be developed or changed quickly), his history and life pattern — all of which are part of his "person."

Back to the Stadium

As the moral focus shifts to the human person, we are not looking at 100,000 abstract dots. We are in the concrete, existential realm: this person, Harry Shoemaker. Human nature, as such, does not exist; only human persons exist. Human nature can be defined in clear and precise terms; human persons cannot. Human nature can be defined in terms of "rational" and "animal." Some clear moral principles about certain activity can be deduced from this fact. But human persons defy categories, are exceedingly complex, and never quite predictable. They cannot be dissociated from background, education, environment, emotions, prejudices, ideals, hopes, dreams, attitudes, character, etc. Human *nature* can be considered apart from the changing aspects of history and culture; human *persons* cannot. Human nature can be understood in itself; human persons cannot exist apart from a web of relationships. Human nature can be considered apart from the influence and the effects of sin; human persons cannot.

But That Leaves So Many Loose Ends!

This change of focus brings out the untidiness and the difficulty of morally evaluating human behavior. It would be so much easier if we could put everyone and every action into "nature" categories, and not have to worry about the personal dimension. Good guy. Bad guy. White hat. Black hat. That's a mortal sin for Joe No. 2. Venial sin for Joe No. 3. This man is a racist, that woman is an adulteress, that teacher is a saint, that mother is totally self-sacrificing. It is relatively easy to identify certain actions as contrary to *nature,* and therefore "evil"; but it is much more difficult to assess the guilt of the unique human person who engages in such activity. Yet, it is only when seen in the light of a particular human person in his total situation that any balanced and full moral judgment can be made as to guilt or praise. Ultimately this is what Scripture means when it says God (and only God) will judge each *person* according to his conduct. So, the change of focus to "person" does make morality more complex and confusing; but it also makes it more realistic and more complete.

The shift in emphasis prompts many agonized questions today. It probably has something to do with some parents complaining that "they don't teach the Ten Commandments any more," and

"Everything's too permissive."

"Father, I was taught it was always a mortal sin to miss Sunday Mass through my own fault. Now my kids tell me that isn't true. Whats' going on?"

"Father, I was told that every deliberate act of impurity is a mortal sin. Is that still true?"

The trouble is that a flat "Yes" or "No" can be misleading, even at times erroneous. There is truth in statements like "Divorce with remarriage is always seriously sinful," and "Missing Mass on Sunday is always a mortal sin." But the statements are made too absolutely, do not allow for special circumstances, and above all put too much stress on isolated and objective actions. They fail to give enough attention to the moral subject, the person. They failed to indicate that a person possibly may *not* be guilty of sin when performing such actions. Failure to indicate this possibility is serious. Focusing on persons makes such ambiguous statements untenable.

The ultimate reason for the shift is the fact that morality has to do with our response to God's call to sonship. Such a call can come only to human persons. The response can be given only by human persons. It must be freely given in the form of love — of which only persons are capable. The response leads to communion — between human beings and between man and God — and to this only *persons* can aspire.

Chapter II

FREEDOM: Not "Doing Whatever You Want," But "Wanting Whatever You Do"

So it's not "man" in general who keeps or breaks the Commandments; it is *this individual* named Harley Combs, or Virginia Schmalzgruber, or Francis X. Nutley III, each a one-of-a-kind, unrepeatable, individual person.

Why are they that way? It's partly physical; no two people on earth, it is said, have the same fingerprints. It's partly historical: no two people on earth have exactly the same history — parents, brothers and sisters, experiences.

But there is a third and much more important element in our uniqueness that determines how much of a real person each of us is: *freedom.*

Only persons can be free, because they alone can make choices in terms of the values they recognize. Only persons can choose which values they prefer, and how they will respond to these values and embody their personal choices in concrete behavior. Only persons can determine what they will

11

become in and through these particular choices and concrete behavior.

Let's see if we all agree on that, before going on.

No other creature below man is free. A leaf does not "freely" float down from the branch where it grew. Every little skipdoodle it takes on the way to earth is completely determined by its weight, air density, air currents. (Any poet reading this is probably appalled to see such a cold-blooded appraisal of that dancing little sacrament of death.) The sunflower doesn't turn to its lord in the west in wide-eyed devotion — it has no choice; it's all physics and chemistry. (Sorry again, Mr. Poet.) Even that highly discriminating sheepdog who "thinks" for your sheep is just a highly-programmed set of instincts. It looks as though he "decides" that this lamb is too far from the flock; his decision to eat or not to eat, to take a leisurely walk in the woods or a nap under the apple tree does not involve calm and prudent reflection: he's programmed — either by built-in instinct or by trained instinct. Clever Hans, the super-horse, doesn't have "horse sense" — he has a memory for signals, especially if the signals include sugar cubes.

Sometimes persons act — or are *made* to act — like dead leaves, sunflowers, circus horses or plow horses. If they do, we speak of them as being "de-personalized" or "de-humanized." Slaves rowing the prison ships might gradually be reduced to the "obedience" of animals — reacting to promise of food. The more one becomes the slave of alcohol or drugs or food or sex, the more one is simply carried away by anger or fear, the less human he is. The man who is made into a cog on someone else's "system," with no chance to participate intelligently, is being de-humanized.

What is the freedom of persons, then? It is the power to "take over" my actions and make them mine. Whether I am St. Francis or Jack the Ripper, what I do is more or less *my* choice. *I* do it. I don't have to do it, I choose to do it. As Father Johann defines it, then, freedom is not doing what I want, but wanting what I do.

(This has limitations, but let's wait a moment before considering them.)

Freedom is the capacity of the human person, in the light of his moral awareness, *to direct himself from within,* from the heart. It is his power to determine how he shall live, to choose the ways in which he expresses values in his actions.

Why are we this way? Because there is a good God who wants to give us the ability to love as he does. And freedom is of the essence of love. God *is* freedom. We are made in his image and likeness.

The more really free we are, the more we are like God; and the freer we are, the more we love, and thus, again, the more we are like God.

Jesus said, "I have come that you may have the truth, and the truth will make you free." Jesus showed us what a truly free man is. He was totally free *from* anybody and anything insofar as these could be hindrances to his total love of the Father. He was free *for* anyone. "Seek first the Kingdom" — that is, open yourself totally to God and his constant activity within your mind and heart. Make

13

God *absolutely* first.

To the degree persons share this freedom, they are not *basically* affected by anything that happens to them. They are not so attached to any person or thing that they cannot find God in its loss. They want to be so un-self-seeking that they can give anyone anything — even their own lives — if that will serve God and man.

The "truth" that Jesus makes us aware of is all reality — the way God is, the deepest meaning of life — in order to liberate us from sin, ignorance and selfishness. He makes it possible for us to choose our attitude, even if we are in a concentration camp, at the mercy of a fatal disease or caught in a human tragedy.

It is in the pursuit and discovery of "truth" that some former supposed "enemies" now find themselves sitting around the same conference table: the psychologist, the Scripture scholar, the philosopher and the theologian. They all agree, from their professional viewpoints, that freedom and truth are at the heart of being a person.

The Scripture scholar sees God and man in relationship as persons; the psychologist helps a man make his own choices in spite of past and present conflicts; the philosopher asks the "why" of life and realizes that the answer is "truth freely lived"; the moral theologian emphasizes that to be moral, to be a person, to be good or evil, is to be a person who takes over his own life and actions in awareness of their meaning.

They all agree that the more free an action is, the more human it is — for good or ill. Without freedom there is no holiness or sin, no love or hate, no heaven or hell.

Wouldn't It Be Better if It Were All Programmed?

It would be so orderly, if you didn't have the messy freedom of life. How beautiful are the feet of the goose-stepping soldiers, how satisfying the football play that "clicks" (like a machine); how predictable the man who "lives like a clock." If God would only program people so that they wouldn't lie or steal or get drunk or take someone else's wife. If all children were only like A-students from the Superdog Obedience School. If someone would only give us a list of exactly what we are supposed to say and do 24 hours a day. It would be so simple.

And so dead. A universe of polished machinery, from which God would turn in boredom. A computer paradise, with no capacity or need to change the program or read the results.

It's a temptation. It's the same lure that drugs offer, or death, or Hitler. "Let me take you over, so you won't have to decide or grow or change or be responsible for your life."

But Isn't It Dangerous?

Some people are afraid that moral theologians go too far in emphasizing freedom today. They fear ending up with a morality of excessive permissiveness, which would contradict both freedom and the Gospel. They remember the traditional morality that did indeed recognize freedom but kept it at a safe distance from the center, like an insecure teacher keeping the extra-bright girl from asking

15

too many questions.

There certainly is risk in seeing freedom as centrally important. Freedom, like love, can be and always has been misunderstood. The notion of freedom can be twisted to mean whatever I want it to mean: "doing what I please," license. St. Paul was aware of the risk of taking on "the yoke of slavery a second time" under the guise of freedom. But he did not stop insisting that we are called to freedom. We dare not sell our human and Christian birthright, the freedom of the children of God, for a "safe" mess of pottage.

For all that, consider who took the biggest risk of all. It is God who puts three billion people on this globe today and says: "I have given you life and intelligence and freedom. I love you and I want you to be with me forever. But you will have to make up your mind to do this freely."

To "decide" is to "cut off." If I make this particular decision for myself, I may never know where another decision might have led. If I decide to go north, I may never know what the path to the south, the east or the west may have brought me.

When I decide anything, I risk misunderstanding, opposition, rejection, suffering. Whatever group of people I join, there is some danger that I may influence them badly or be badly influenced by them.

But it is an equally bad decision if I decide not to decide. If I hang back from life, wait to be forced, then I am making the most immoral of decisions — I am refusing the talent God gave me. I am burying it because "I knew you were a severe man, etc."

The one risk I may not take is to be non human, not a person, not one who thinks, pursues value and seeks for meaning, takes over his own life, loves freely. This is the worst immorality. It is to fail the *greatest commandment* which must obviously come before the Ten — to give and spend our lives totally and lovingly in the service of God and man. Without freedom this is impossible. The less free we are, the less we can fulfill the greatest commandment — or even the least. Moral evil, sin, is refusing to determine myself in a way that promotes my own personal growth and the good of others.

The Inevitable Limitations of Freedom

But we need to be realists as well as idealists. Let us admit that freedom is not the same in everyone.

Personal freedom is limited by many circumstances. First, by a lack of *knowledge*. If I have not been taught to read, I can be "turned loose" in the best library in the world and I might as well be in prison as far as reading *Hamlet* or the *Gettysburg Address* is concerned. I am *potentially* free to do these things, but not *actually*. I can't do what I do not know about: I can't mean what I do not understand.

My freedom can be diminished or taken away by *emotion, passion*. I may be so paralyzed with fear, or "out of my mind" with anger or grief that I do not really make the vow, or pronounce a curse, with any real freedom. I am "carried away." It would seem that there is a certain amount of "force" from emotion in all we do. Emotions can enhance and intensify our free choices (e.g., to pray fervently), or diminish our freedom (e.g., to discuss while angry). To grow in freedom means to channel these emotional forces in the direction we choose — like a fireman getting the water on the actual fire, instead of letting the powerful firehose flap about aimlessly.

Third, my freedom is limited by my circumstances. Right now I am in so much pain, or I am so tired, that I *cannot* concentrate on listening to the news, meditating on the Gospel or saying the rosary. Or, if I have always lived in the most gracious circumstances, I simply cannot live in the squalor, hunger, cold and despair of the slum.

My freedom is limited by my temperament. If I am the "picture-straightener" type, I cannot relax with a pinochle game 15 minutes before the crucial meeting, like my easy-going friend. And if I'm the scrupulous, indecisive type, you may have to almost drag some decisions out of me.

The list could be continued — parents, birthplace, culture, education, my personal history. My freedom can be limited *to a degree* by these various circumstances. But it is not all black and white; it's not that we are simply free (100 per cent), or not. We are free, but "more or less" free. Because this is so, our moral responsibility is also "more or less" limited.

But our glory is that we *are* free, modest though that freedom is. Our privilege *and our vocation* is that we can grow to becoming more and more free. Perhaps that child walking into the library *will* someday be able to *choose* to read *Hamlet* or the *Gettysburg Address.* I *can* gradually work through my fear and anger. I *can* gradually come to terms with the difficulty of living in the slum.

Or I may decide to remain stunted and enslaved.

Our challenge at every step of the way is to assume the direction of our life as well as we *can,* and to grow in that potentially almost unlimited freedom. Freedom is our life task as human persons. We are called to share as fully as possible the liberation Christ won for us. Slowly, gradually, we are to become mature, i.e., persons who act in the light of truth and want what they do.

The greatest limitation of freedom comes from sin. Every sin dims the light in our life a little bit. Every sin chills our relationship with God and with others a little bit. If the darkness and the cold increase, we become more and more rigid, fixed on a path which we know leads to destruction but to which we increasingly enslave ourselves.

The sinner is caught in a vicious circle of his own making. The more he rejects God, the more he damages the health of his personality: his clear vision of reality, his ability to choose according to truth. The more he ruins his thinking-deciding ability, the less ugly and tragic sin appears to him. His very freedom is responsible for his loss of freedom.

Though the internal damage to freedom in any person is the most tragic result of sin, we cannot fail to note also how sin limits the freedom of others. The sinfulness of a city government that denies good education to the poor is limiting the freedom of the poor. My prejudice towards blacks limits their freedom through my voting habits, my influence on others, my refusal to cooperate in integration. Parents who poison the atmosphere of their homes with greed, selfishness, bickering, are denying their children the atmosphere in which their personalities can grow in freedom.

Sin in the world, sin in the institutions of society, sin in our parents, sin in ourselves — all sin limits our freedom. All of us are more or less sinful ourselves, and more or less influenced by the sinfulness of others. Accordingly all of us are limited in our freedom.

This may sound pessimistic. It is not meant to be. It is intended to underscore a basic fact of life. There is sin, and therefore there is slavery to sin to a greater or lesser degree, and slavery to the effects of sin.

We have stressed the limitations of freedom in order to come to a more realistic approach to morality. It is not true that every one of those 100,000 dots in the stadium is simply "free." Each one of them is "more or less" free, and the judgment of their goodness or badness can be made only in the light of that reality.

So, freedom is a task, as well as a "given." It is not something to be presumed in perfect condition, so that the main emphasis can then be on what is *done. Becoming* free is part of the process. Morality is not just what we *do;* it is the way we freely express ourselves.

In short, we have to "free" our freedom itself.

It will be as difficult as Michelangelo's "freeing" that statue of Moses from the block of marble dragged into his studio. Just as hard, and just as glorious.

Chapter III

RESPONSIBILITY:
Please Drive
Carefully

the men who roar past the Indianapolis fans at 200 miles an hour nurse their Mustangs along at 20 miles per hour in school zones. If they drive the Chicago expressways, they watch for the monitors above their lane and keep their cars within the parallel white lines, switching lanes only when their experience tells them there is enough time and space, and with a careful flickering of turn signals. If they drive alone in a heavy truck over grazing ranges in Texas, they may drive almost anywhere they please, if there are no people, cattle or oil wells around.

An ambulance driver bringing in the critically wounded takes a certain amount of risk as he crosses intersections. He trusts other motorists' eyes and ears to hear his siren and see the flashing light. A policeman pursuing a fleeing criminal takes risks that he would not chance if he were driving his family on Sunday afternoon.

A student driver doesn't turn into traffic until there almost *isn't* any traffic.

Freedom in a human being is more powerful, for good or ill, than all the horsepower beneath the hoods of automobiles. It can speed people to holiness, carry them safely through storms or bear them along quietly in prayer; it can also plunge them over moral cliffs and bring them to smash themselves to pieces in moral violence.

Come to think of it, "auto-mobile" means "self-moving"; freedom is my real but limited power to determine my path. Responsibility is the path chosen. Freedom and responsibility involve the same power seen from different perspectives. Freedom refers to *me* as the source of my life, my actions; responsibility refers to *other person(s)* to whom my life, my actions are directed.

We can make the mistake about automobiles that we sometimes make in speaking about freedom. Freedom *can* be described as the power to do anything you please, any time, any place, any way. An automobile *can* be driven at any speed, almost any place, any time, any way.

This is "raw" freedom, freedom that contains within itself the possibility of abuse. It's like the power in the atom, which *can* be used to kill every person in New York. It's like the muscular power of a mother or father, who *could* deprive their baby of life if they chose.

There would be no heroes if it were impossible to be a coward; there would be no saints if it were impossible to sin. Still, the abuse of freedom is the death of freedom. To escape the "slavery" of total love is to become bound in the slavery of self-ishness. The tragedy of mortal sinfulness is that I destroy my person and my freedom by abusing my person and my freedom.

I can use my Ford to get into the house without using the door, if I want to. It can take me from the top of the cliff to the bottom of the canyon in a few seconds, if that's the way I choose to go. It will help me get through a crowd of sluggish pedestrians in almost no time. But that's not what Henry Ford had in mind.

Freedom is freedom only when it's used for its purpose — to relate to others in giving and receiving, and through them to God. As the song goes, a song is not a song until you sing it, a bell is not a bell until you ring it. Freedom is not free unless we "free" it — for others.

Funny thing about words. Usage coats over the original meaning. Our word "respond" comes from a Latin word which meant "to *promise* in return." In our own Anglo-Saxon past, the word "answer" meant "to *swear* against." In either case, the response or answer is not just *any* kind of answer, but a serious, truthful, real one, to another person. A responsible person is one who uses his freedom to be in serious, truthful, real relationship to others. It is impossible to separate the realities symbolized by the words "person," "freedom," "responsibility," and "morality." To be moral is to be responsible; to be a person is to be free; to be free is to be responsible.

Very often we think of "responsibility" as "liability for punishment." "Who's responsible for this accident?" "Who's responsible for this mess?" But that's the question of a judge. There's a more positive meaning of "responsible" which is the decision of a person about himself: "I will take over my action freely. It will be mine — my choice, my determination. Not forced upon me, but my choice. I want what I do." Even this can be "raw" freedom and not yet real: a thief can fully take over his action, in this sense. But when we join this idea of responsibility to the need of relating to others in serious and truthful giving and receiving, we have the full picture of man as God made him to be: a person who makes his life his own and chooses to *be* somebody in relationship to other persons and ultimately to God.

If responsibility is seen in this full and broad sense, it is seen to embrace all we are and all our activity, all morality.

This can be spelled out in three statements, which may help to clarify our notion of responsibility.

1. *We are responsible not only for our actions, but for our selves.* This means: "I take over, I make completely my own, not just my external and individual *actions,* but my *self,* what I *am.*" Responsibility involves praying or eating or working, not lying or stealing or hurting someone. It involves relating to others with care and patience and understanding. Responsibility means all this, but it means much more. These are outward expressions of responsibility. Beneath all these expressions, responsibility involves what I do with my *self,* my stance in life, the *whole* of me. Responsibility

means, at its core, my ability to shape my *self*.

In other words, in all of my particular choices, in all the concrete ways I choose to act or not to act there are *two* aspects: I am performing some concrete action, and I am expressing my *self* in that action. My activity is given a particular outward (bodily) expression; in and through that outward expression I am shaping my *self*. In so doing I am shaping my *life*.

Thus when I choose to be moderate in drinking, not to accept a bribe, to march in a demonstration for civil rights — I am determining the shape of my outward behavior, but I am also expressing my self and determining the *kind of person I am becoming*. Responsibility, in its full sense, embraces an inner and an outer aspect. Responsibility involves not only what I do, but more, *who I am*.

2. *Therefore freedom and responsibility have to do with more than laws, commandments.* Laws are a facet of morality, but they are not morality. Laws are like the boundary lines of a football field, or the "works" of a telephone. Laws are like the banks of a river or the keyboard of a piano. There is always something deeper and bigger involved, a purpose and meaning, values and goals, people.

Today, in panic at the abuse of freedom (something in which God takes the basic risk) many would like to reduce morality (and responsibility) to the observance of law. You are a responsible citizen if you obey the laws and pay your taxes. You are a responsible student if you study the lessons the teacher assigns. You are a responsible person if you keep the Commandments: you do not kill, commit adultery, steal, slander or covet; you do what you are told; you don't use God's name in vain; you have no other gods (though this last is a bit hazy!). You are a responsible Catholic if you go to Mass on Sunday, put your envelope in the collection basket, refrain from meat on seven Fridays of the year, fast on Ash Wednesday and Good Friday, and obey other detailed laws of the Church, especially those that tell you what not to do. Now, this obedience to laws, especially laws that prohibit something, is an *aspect* of responsibility. But it is by no means the whole of it. Thus to restrict responsibility would be tragic.

The laws of the Church, and the laws of our country, especially the negative ones, are important only *in terms of greater value.* Thus, traffic laws are important insofar as they promote social order and safeguard life and property. Laws prohibiting theft, libel, murder are important because they involve basic rights of persons and seek to maintain safety, peace, and harmony among persons in society.

But, laws which prohibit or prescribe certain actions involve only a small part of our lives. *There is a greater part of my life in which no particular law tells me what to do or not do.* There is so much to me, so many of my activities that such concrete laws do not and cannot regulate; e.g., what I will do with this free afternoon, what present I will give my family for Christmas, what major I will pursue in college, what books I will read, etc. Yet in the *whole* of my life, in *all* my behavior, I am called to express myself freely, called to love God and neighbor. No concrete "laws" can ever embrace the whole of my life. What is more, my very obedience to these concrete laws must be evaluated and shaped by this deeper understanding of responsibility. By far the most important and basic "laws" are the positive and open-ended "laws," such as "be merciful," "be honest," "be truthful," "love your neighbor as yourself."

3. *The responsible freedom of persons is on-going,* dynamic. It is not a static, once-and-for-all matter. No one can say he "learned his religion" in grade school or high school or college or marriage or business or when he was 71 years old. To be a person, to be responsible, is to *answer (respond)* as God calls to us in all the unfolding circumstances of our life. I cannot look at any act of mine *in isolation from all my other actions.* I cannot consider the "outside" of my life in isolation from the "inside" of my life. I cannot consider my life in isolation from other persons — God and man. I cannot consider my present life in isolation from the past or the future. To be a free and responsible human person is to be *growing toward wholeness* and fulfill-ment. Or, as St. Paul says, we are "to form that perfect man who is Christ come to full stature" (Ephesians 4,13).

Responsibility ultimately has to do with the on-going attitude of our life as a whole: the whole moving river, not just some apparently isolated cur-rents, colors or floating debris. At the heart of life and morality is our ability to shape our *selves.* Ac-cordingly, we cannot really understand, much less morally evaluate, anyone's outward behavior unless we know his inner attitudes and dispositions, the overall direction and orientation he is giving his life.

For example, if we wanted to make a *complete* moral evaluation of the conduct of two people, we would have to possess a knowledge that belongs only to God. We can, indeed, deal with externals. We can make an "objective" evaluation. If John and Mary, who are soon to be married, engage in premarital intercourse, we can say: 1) They are not married. 2) Intercourse is licit only for married persons. 3) Therefore, they have done something that is against God's law, and is called fornication.

There is truth here, of course. The conclusion does follow from the premises. This approach does enable us to say *something* about the moral meaning of a particular instance of human activity. But there is so much this approach does *not* enable us to say. It does not enable us to understand what really happened between John and Mary. It does not enable us to understand the *moral significance* of this act of John and Mary and its bearing on their relationship with one another, with others and with God. To evaluate this act in terms of moral responsibility, we would have to look at it in terms of their relationship (engaged) and in terms of what preceded it and what is foreseen to follow upon it. We have to look at this act in terms of who John and Mary are, the *kind of persons* they are, their *attitudes* and *character,* the way they *usually* express themselves, their intentions, their motives, the over-all direction of their lives and above all their basic relationship to God. It is only by moving in this direction that we can evaluate morally what *they* did and so see their action in its full moral perspective.

It should go without saying that it is practically impossible to make this kind of moral judgment about anyone but ourselves. "Do not judge." Our point here is that the morality of free responsible human persons is a matter of their *whole* persons.

Freedom, then, is at the heart of all morality. The human person is born with the capacity to determine himself, gradually to shape the direction of his life in and through all the particular choices whereby he expresses his response to men and so to God. The human person is subject to many influences, pressures and forces. His freedom is very limited. Yet, it is out of such freedom that his moral responsibility springs. Insofar as he is free, he is responsible, not only in isolated actions but also in his real ability to determine himself in a basic way. This is most especially true in the way he relates to other human persons, builds community and so loves God. Thus, morality is responsibility, and freedom is its source.

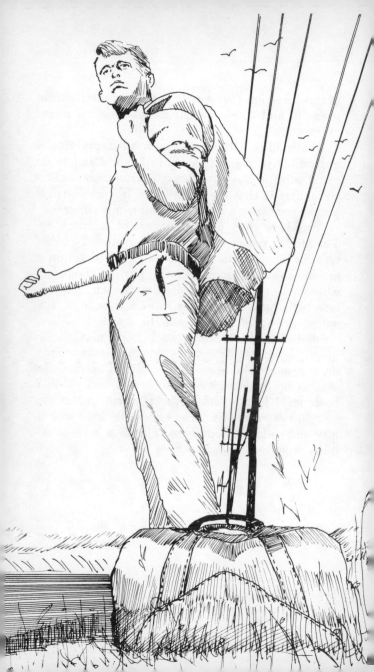

Chapter IV

MORTAL SIN: You Can't Run away from Home All at Once

Some days you can't make a nickel, even in kindergarten. Michael Joseph Armbruster, with six full years of life behind him, came to that conclusion very suddenly. It happened the day the sandbox was damp, the movie projector broke, the teacher made them take a nap, and Susie Bader was sick in front of the teacher's desk. Reaching home, he was confronted with the situation of having to stay indoors because of his cold, do without a coke, straighten up his toys, and listen to screechy-voiced Linda Bailey play cards with his sister. When he found his piggy bank broken on the floor, with none of its contents in sight, he realized that the camel's back was indeed broken. Only drastic measures could solve the life-crisis into which he had fallen.

He took a small blanket from his bed, two socks, a small flashlight and his baseball bat, bundled them together and marched into the kitchen to break the news to his mother.

"I'm going to run away from home," he said, "and I'm not coming back." It didn't sound quite right. So he added, — *"except for meals."*

Michael Joseph Armbruster is as far as he can be from the attitude of a Judas or a St. John, or that of his father and mother. He is a person, but he is not yet free and responsible enough to take his whole life into his hands and place it unreservedly on the side of good or evil, God or mammon.

Where and when and how will he cross that mysterious line (if indeed it is a line) that separates the men from the boys? When is he deep enough, how long must he grow, to make a mature and definite stand about being either with Christ or against him?

To put the question in another way, what is this fatal disease that so pervades a person's life that it is called "mortal" sinfulness? In contrast, what is the mind and heart of mature Christian men and women who have given their lives to Christ totally?

It is obvious that there is no mortal sinfulness in Michael's childish "rebellion." Mortal sinfulness could be more exactly compared to Michael's father's running away from home, first by months and years of growing indifference, neglect and selfishness, and finally by the overt act of a carefully planned "running" off with another woman.

Mortal sinfulness is just such a leaving of our Father's house. Like the Prodigal Son, we take our whole inheritance with us to squander. It is being willing to leave the father's table for good. It is no whim of the moment, but a decision about life. The father, as it were, formally accepts the son's decision to abandon home; he puts the whole inheritance check in his hands. They both know what will be done with it. The father weeps, but he does not stop his son. Staying home must be a choice, not a chore.

Today we are asking the question which seemed to be answered very clearly in our catechism, but which has engaged the most strenuous thought of theologians and saints through the centuries. What is grace? What is sin? It's not that the catechism definition is wrong; but it's only the tip of the iceberg: six-sevenths of it is under water. What, indeed, is "full knowledge," "full consent"? What is *"serious matter"*?

People today are again raising fundamental questions of morality. Neither Scripture, nor the Church, nor theologians have the complete answer. There is much we know, but there is much we do not know. Even in our enlightened 20th century, sin and grace remain a mystery.

New insights, however, are being discussed and are worth our study. Morality as presented by many Catholic theologians today approaches sin in a way different from that of the old catechisms.

Knowing the Disease from Its Opposite: Grace

Death is meaningless except in terms of life. A corpse is a tragedy only because life is so beautiful. Only living people can weep over a dead body; they know the tragedy of the total loss of that deep and precious current called life.

So it is with mortal sinfulness. It can be described only in terms of its opposite. It is a nothingness where once there was something beautiful. It is emptiness where there was fullness. It is total and continuing separation, where once there was continuing union.

At the heart of our life is grace. We have a Father who out of pure graciousness freely calls us to life in Jesus by means of his Spirit. Human life, in God's eternal intention, was to be life in Christ, sonship. God never had any plans for a merely "natural" man or woman.

To be "graced" by God means that his own life flows in our person like blood, like spirit. We are living branches grafted onto the living Vine who is Christ. We are, in the daring phrase of Paul, his *members* — eyes, ears, hands, feet. We are taken into God's family while remaining uniquely ourselves. We become more fully human as we become more fully alive in Christ.

Because this is something between persons, we call it what any "something between persons" is called: *a relationship* — a case of "you can't have one without the other," as the song says. A man is a husband only and precisely because he has a wife. I can't be a giver if there are no receivers; I can't receive if no one gives.

So our grace-life is a two-way street, a relationship; we inhale God's life and exhale love.

Grace cannot be a *something,* just as the love of husband and wife is not a something stored in a vault. Grace is not a static, motionless thing, like the house I live in. It is not a marriage record, or a report card, or a computer read-out. It is persons freely giving and receiving each other's love in an ongoing relationship.

In calling us, the Father is not an employer who needs a certain number of apples picked in his orchard. He doesn't want to *use* us for anything. He is a lover who wants our whole heart — for our sake and for his sake; not selfishly or tyrannically, but because that is the only way to man's fulfillment and God's glory. *To accept or reject this relationship is "serious matter."*

Mortal Sinfulness

The most amazing thing about mortal sinfulness is the very fact that it is even *possible*. How can anyone, in his right mind, reject Love itself? Sin is possible because God took the biggest risk of all. He had to give man *"raw"* freedom if there was ever going to be *loving* freedom.

In one way or another we have always said this, but we vastly over-simplified matters, and this led to distortion and confusion about mortal sin. The traditional requirements for mortal sin — serious matter, full knowledge, full freedom — are easy to memorize, but extremely difficult to apply. Children, teenagers, even adults can and do perform actions that are wrong, even gravely wrong. But to conclude that they are guilty of mortal sin is quite another matter. To say a child has sufficient moral awareness and personal freedom to commit a mortal sin is nonsense. It is difficult to know when a teenager is sufficiently mature, appreciative of moral values, and sufficiently free to make the profound decision required for mortal sin.

What must mortal sinfulness be? Nothing less than the rejection of the graced-relationship with the Father. Sin is the fully conscious and free refusal of the Father's offer of a life relationship of love given and received; or, what is even more mysterious, the cold-blooded abandonment of such a relationship once it has been entered into.

It is not necessary that the sinner make an explicit statement or intention that he "wants to reject God." But in order that he be guilty of a willful turning away from God, he has to be aware that this is what he is doing. It is implicit in his totally selfish love of himself.

This basic rejection takes shape in and underlies any individual "act" of mortal sinfulness. It is indeed a refusal to *do* something; but it is first a refusal to *be* something.

Obviously such a decision must be *personal*. Only a Harry Shoemaker or a Molly Johnson is capable of personal relationship or personal rejection of it. There is no reservoir of corruption called mortal sin, somehow able to suck people into death; there is no vast warehouse of grace in heaven, from which suitable portions are sent to holy addresses. Mortal sin is vacuum that a man produces at the heart of his own life. It is nothingness, absence, loss, the rigidity of a corpse. Because it is *mortal*, such a refusal must involve an awareness and freedom that is in proportion to the seriousness of extinguishing a relationship with God. It is basic, and it is something that happens only gradually. Only a relatively mature person is really capable of mortal sin.

To be sure, *evil* exists in our lives. But *guilt* is quite another matter, especially the guilt of mortal sinfulness. Guilt has to do with our inner relationship with God. *Real* guilt does not necessarily have anything to do with an *external* "guilt" that courts of law must deal with. It may be easy to prove that a man performed a series of actions which are labeled "crime" in the law; it is impossible for a court of law to know of a man's relationship with God.

New Morality and Sin

Although a surprising number of people seem to imply it, theologians never taught that you could commit a mortal sin without *knowing* it, without realizing the basic *meaning* of what you were doing. You cannot be taken by surprise in mortal sin. One of the requirements for mortal sin is full knowledge or awareness. Also, theologians have always stressed that full freedom was necessary for a person to be guilty of mortal sin. Although they never quite indicated what they meant by full freedom, they did admit that fear, passion, compulsive habit, ignorance could be of such force that even such gravely evil actions as killing and adultery would not be mortally sinful as far as the interior guilt of a person was concerned.

The newer approach to morality maintains that a person cannot commit a mortal sin "out of the blue"; moreover, that a person cannot commit a mortal sin in any single isolated act.

Notice we are not saying a person cannot *do* something wrong, even seriously wrong, in one single act, e.g., fornication. We are not saying that a single act, taken in itself, cannot have serious and harmful consequences, e.g., a lie that ruins a reputation. We are not saying a person cannot act rather suddenly and cause dreadful harm to himself or others, e.g., a killing. Our concern here is mortal sin, personal guilt.

Our question is: What must be involved if a person is to be *guilty* interiorly of a mortal sin? That is: If a person is basically reversing his relationship with God in the process of *doing* what is morally wrong, what must be his awareness and interior decision? Our assertion is that a person cannot be *guilty* of such a mortal sin — changing his basic relationship to God — in a single, *isolated* action, no matter how serious is the moral evil of *what* he does. Our contention is that human persons come only *gradually* to the point of sufficient moral awareness and moral freedom as to be able to change basically their relationship with God. Let's look at this more closely.

Individual human *actions,* as such, are of short duration. I may read or walk or meditate or work or talk. I may curse or drink or lie or fornicate or kill. What we *do* is done rather quickly. But the point to be stressed is this: mature personal decisions involving grave matter and serious consequences are *not* reached quickly. It is only gradually that I come to an awareness of the values, alternatives, consequences involved in a particular kind of situation. How slowly it begins to dawn on so many smokers that there is really a link between smoking and cancer. How ill-advised and impulsive we con-

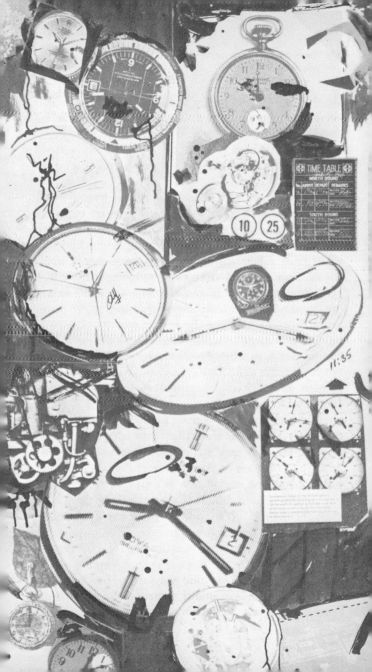

sider a man who hastily makes a big decision involving serious consequences. No doubt we *can,* and do, make serious decisions quickly. The point is we cannot make *mature* decisions about serious matters quickly. Sufficient awareness takes a lot of time.

Secondly, as with moral awareness so also with free decisions. It is only gradually that we come to the point of maturely and freely determining ourselves in serious ways that affect our whole life. We experience many influences and constraints from within and without (habits, attitudes, fears, society, Church, family, circumstances, etc.). When we are faced with a serious matter that is going to have grave consequences for the rest of our lives, we just have to take time to work through to a decision. We cannot reach mature decisions suddenly when important values are at stake, various alternatives are present and serious consequences hang in the balance.

Circumstances at times force us to make big decisions quickly. If such decisions turn out well, it is because we were "lucky," or because we drew heavily upon past experience and decisions which did involve time and study. We simply are not acting maturely and freely if we make big decisions "out of the blue." If we do, we are considered childish, immature, imprudent. In coming to important decisions we "feel our way"; we search, grope, probe, take tentative steps, try out smaller decisions, take a position one way and then another way. But gradually, as our awareness of what is at stake and what are the consequences becomes clear, we come to the point where we firmly choose our course of action. We gradually take our stand, make our choice and express our choice in behavior.

Consider an example: Steve is 25, has a loving wife and three children, lives in suburbia, has a good job and works hard at Radar, Inc. He has ordinarily been honest, but he loves money and spends freely. When he becomes a junior executive, Steve begins to change. He discovers how to cut corners and make an easy but dishonest dollar. The more he gets away with, the more he wheels and deals. Easy come, easy go. He begins to spend money as fast as he makes it. He always needs more. So his life becomes a process of finding new ways of getting it.

There are times along the way, especially in the beginning, when Steve is aware of what is happening, aware that his honesty, integrity, respect for the rights of others, concern for family are gradually slipping away. There are times when Steve is aware of the *pattern* that is developing. But he goes on making more deals, using more people to achieve his goals. More and more he becomes absorbed in "business," as he now sees it, and less concerned about family and friends. He wants to be president of the company. He trains himself to be hard, relentless, ruthless. His whole life is swept along in his single passion; money, prestige, power become overriding concerns of his life. Everyone and everything else take second place.

Steve is changing his basic orientation. The fact that he has long since rejected God *interiorly* —

that he is guilty of mortal sinfulness — will be fi-
-nalized *even outwardly.* It may be through a lie
that ruins another man's career; by adultery; by
cooperation in violence. But mortal sinfulness has
gradually come to exist before the externalizing of
its presence. *Mortal sinfulness takes shape in and
underlies the single, isolated, evil act.*

In our really serious moral decisions something
similar happens. Murder, fornication, lying and
stealing with serious consequences, etc., can happen quickly. But, moral guilt for such actions depends on awareness of the moral values at stake
and personal free decision. Those, we maintain,
cannot come quickly. Every mature moral decision
is interrelated with other moral decisions of the
past and with awareness of moral values. The
whole process develops only gradually; it cannot
happen in one single, isolated action.

It is for reasons such as these that we maintain
an *orientation morality.* Our lives are "of a piece,"
one whole. We grow slowly and hesitantly. We
come to decisions, especially important decisions,
slowly and almost always with doubts and trepida-
tions. We come finally but gradually to a basic orientation of our life, for good or evil. We do not zig-
zag quickly or easily between grace and mortal sin,
like skiers weaving between poles.

Another example: John and Mary have been
married for 10 years. If they have not been communicating for years, if their quarrels have gotten
more and more bitter and unresolved, if any real
concern for each other has slowly evaporated, then
they have gradually destroyed the life of their mar-

riage. They have made a basic, fundamental life-decision that cannot be separated from their relationship to God. The final destruction of their relationship may take the form of adultery and divorce. These are not sudden and isolated actions. They are the *expression* of an interior attitude that has been formed by countless individual decisions.

Something very similar must take place if anyone is ever to reach the condition of being "in" mortal sin. The decision to change one's way of life basically, passing from grace to mortal sin, happens only gradually.

The new moral approach (orientation) stresses that for a person to be "guilty of mortal sin," a basic change must occur in the *person*. To say a person has "committed mortal sin" is to say that he has behaved outwardly in a way that *manifests inward rejection* of God. That is really what mortal sin is; that is really what the requirement of full knowledge and full freedom is about.

So, the most important question is not *what* was done, but what was the disposition of the *person* in and through the action. The behavior, the action, is ambiguous. As such, it may or may not reflect what really occurs in the person. A person can *do* something and still maintain his basic relationship with God; e.g., a homosexual, despite sincere efforts, engages in a morally evil sexual act. *Actions* can be seriously wrong, but the person may not be mortally guilty.

Taking Venial Sinfulness Seriously

We are not implying that persons are not guilty

at all of their morally evil actions. It is the presence of *mortal* guilt that is being questioned. Having argued this, we would argue just as strongly that personal guilt (something less than mortal, yet real guilt) should not be minimized. Indeed, perhaps if we can free ourselves of an *excessive* preoccupation with mortal sin and all its many paralyzing ramifications and fears, we may well be in a position to take our real guilt more seriously and deal with it more effectively.

We may then begin to realize that the terrible harm and suffering in the world — apathy, greed, cruelty, injustice, deprivation, etc. — are the result of our actions, our behavior, and we are guilty. We may become more aware of the social harm caused by our personal sins. We may be much less inclined to play down venial sins and assume responsibility for our real guilt, such as it is, and really endeavor to change our lives and behavior for the better (convert!).

On the other hand, if we are nearer the truth in believing that persons are seldom guilty of mortal sin, we have much greater reason to be *hopeful*. We can live in hope and not in fear of the ever-present danger of suddenly "falling into mortal sin" and going to hell. We can trust in the power and goodness of God, which does not seem too credible if so many people are committing mortal sins so frequently!

We can have a more optimistic belief in the power of Jesus' death and resurrection in transforming our lives. We can put greater hope and trust in the basic goodness and sincerity of people who want to lead decent lives. We can find hope for those who are caught in the web of illicit sex, alcohol and drugs.

Finally, if, as we have argued, persons are seldom guilty of mortal sin, this in no way minimizes the importance or necessity of the sacrament of confession. The orientation approach applies to conversion as well as to sin. Just as a person only gradually comes to change his life in a sinful way, so also does he only gradually change his life in genuine conversion. We are guilty and in need of forgiveness for *all* our sins. To say that confession is "necessary" only for mortal sin is to dilute the meaning of the sacrament. In the sacrament of reconciliation, free and responsible Christians *celebrate* the power of God's mercy to heal them as persons, in their *whole* lives. It is a hopeful expression of willingness to strive, within this power of God, to transform their very lives.

For good or ill, our lives move toward becoming more and more a basic decision for God or for evil. The channel grows deeper as the river flows.

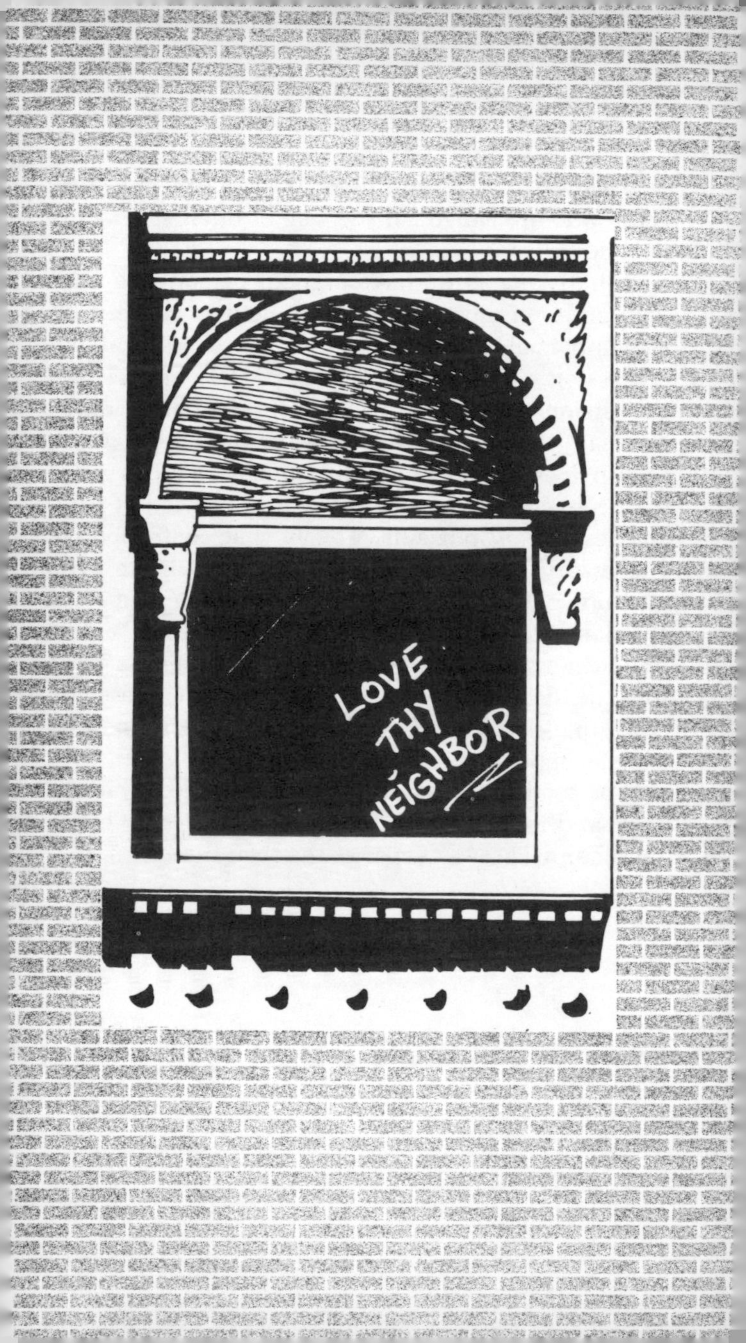
LOVE
THY
NEIGHBOR

Chapter V

ACCENTUATE
THE POSITIVE

et's be fair to the Baltimore Catechism. It was
not written — could not have been written — for
the exploding world culture in which Catholics
live today. It should not be unduly blamed for the
strongly negative morality that has seemed to characterize American Catholicism.

In its section on the Commandments, 10 of the
97 pages are devoted to the two "Great Commandments"; more than half of this space treats the
seven corporal and spiritual works of mercy — certainly a major and beautiful element in the lives of
countless Catholics. In the section on the Ten Commandments, the overall treatment (judging by the
amount of space used) is slightly more negative
than positive. In the treatment of the first four
Commandments, the ratio is 60 per cent positive
and 40 per cent negative. In the remaining six
Commandments, the ratio is 30 per cent positive
and 70 per cent negative.

So there was a strong emphasis on the positive, especially in the Great Commandments of love. For God and our parents we did learn more things *to do* than not to do.

But we did learn (in catechisms, at least) more things *not to do in the areas covered by the last six Commandments* — "after" God and home, so to speak. Perhaps this is one source of that strange paradox in American Catholic life: on the one hand, great faith, generosity, loyalty to the Church; and on the other, a very legalistic and negative conception of vast areas of social relationships.

The impression was given, whether rightly or not, that being Catholic meant there were a lot of things you *couldn't* do. (Many people thought, and some still do think, that this "strictness" of the Church was its greatest asset.) Many of us grew into adulthood knowing many ways of sinning by being dishonest, but appreciating too little the implications of justice and its concrete expression in our lives. We were hyper-aware of the many ways of being unchaste but scarcely conscious of the positive values of sexuality and chastity.

Allied with this negative emphasis was a certain lack of trust in ourselves and others. It wasn't exactly said in so many words, but there was a strong implication that we were dangerous bundles of evil inclinations. Given an inch of rope, we would surely hang ourselves in mortal sin. Michael Joseph Armbruster had emotions, but they would probably go the wrong way. And Harry Shoemaker had better be careful about how he looks at that girl next to him, even if she's covered with six blankets. True, God created our bodies and our emotions, but only our "souls" were completely trustworthy.

Stress on perfect control of the senses, preoccupation with avoiding temptation, fleeing the occasions of sin, led to an understanding of Christian life that could be quite distorted — even though accompanied by generous love and an almost heroic exercise of those corporal and spiritual works of mercy. The distortion expressed itself most cruelly in the scrupulosity that consumed endless days of worry (and hours in the confessional) and all sorts of feelings of *false guilt* undiscernibly tangled with real. It was not surprising that a great number of people suffered the deepest trauma of all: "I am no good. I am worthless. I cannot love, because I have nothing to give. I am not worth being loved."

A third aspect of this negative approach of the past is the fact that it kept many Catholic adults in a state of moral childishness. They learned well the sins, the prohibitions, the occasions of sins. But they knew little of the underlying reasons why sins were sins. They came into adulthood with little understanding and appreciation of the positive values of Catholic living. They could firmly and surely lay down the law to their children; they could clearly and securely tell their teenage sons and daughters what not to do. But when their children and teenagers began to ask "why," they were very much at a loss. The same deficiency in maturity is clearly apparent in two other phenomena of Catholic life: the readiness of adults, parents, to ask priests for quick "answers," and the childish way in which

51

very many adults go to confession.

The fourth aspect of this negative approach of the past is manifested in the lack of *social* moral consciousness. It is relatively simple to set down very concrete rules about what I should not do to others — a tendency that leads to a rather individualistic and minimalistic morality. I should not kill others, cheat others, lie to others. I should not fornicate or commit adultery with others. I should not ruin their good name. It is easy to conclude that I am "keeping the commandments" by *not* hurting others. (A parish missionary relates that he always had difficulty, in visiting classrooms during missions, getting the kids to say what you *"do* do" to keep the commandments, not just what you "don't do.")

Even pursuing this negative mentality, I can hurt my neighbor by more ways than slander, seduction and stealing. I hurt him even if he doesn't realize it, by not giving him the attention, help, encouragement that he needs.

Morality is also a question of what I positively do for God, for my neighbor and for myself. How do I treat my neighbor with respect and honesty in all the complications of today's business world? How do I love my national and world neighbors *justly* in the midst of desperate poverty, substandard housing, racial discrimination, unequal education and employment? What do you do?

The newer, more positive, and *far more demanding* emphasis in morality has grown out of recent research in Scripture, theology, philosophy and psychology. It involves the change of focus from nature to person and a greater emphasis on freedom and responsibility. The present emphasis is on "doing good." In the past it was, "Be careful, watch for temptation, avoid risk." The emphasis in the present is "Don't just sit there. *Do* something! Get involved!" (Without forgetting the need for contemplation as expressed in the reverse of this advise: "Don't just do something — sit there!") The emphasis in the past involved suspicion, mistrust and a pessimistic view of man as ever on the verge of sin. Think especially of our mistrust of our feelings, especially of our sexual feelings.

The emphasis in the present — with due awareness of our sinful condition — is one of trust and encouragement. This places much more hope in the power of the saving death of Jesus and the grace of his Spirit in our lives. It has much more confidence in the goodness and sincerity of human persons who share in the risen life of Jesus.

"Accentuate the positive! Do good!" is much more in harmony with the Gospel: "Love one another as I have loved you." "He went about doing good." "By this shall all men know you are my disciples, if you love one another."

In our terms, this says: Grow up! Don't stand around all your life in the paralysis of fear of sin. TRUST YOURSELF, for you have been touched by Christ's powerful redeeming love. Trust in him and get going, get involved. When we come down to it, we have just so much energy. We can get caught up in a paralysis of fear, or we can get caught up in spending our energy in loving others. It seems obvious that the best way to avoid evil is to do good.

Perhaps all this sounds too optimistic, unrealistic, even naive. It may seem to smack of an un-Christian disregard for evil and the sinfulness of men. But there seems to be no other way to properly estimate the presence and power of Jesus in our lives. Sin is real and powerful, but the Gospel reveals a Jesus who is more real and more powerful (Romans 5).

We are all sinners, we are all sinful. We are all weak and imperfect. We never measure up to our potential. Our attitudes and behavior often leave much to be desired. We are frequently confused in our ideas and our goals. We are even more frequently confused and mixed-up in our feelings and emotions. We often find it difficult to relate fruitfully with other persons. We often are careless or negligent, preoccupied or indifferent, lazy, vacillating not only in terms of our duties but also in the countless opportunities to love and be of service to other persons.

This is to admit that there can be much more "venial" sinfulness in our lives than we care to admit — the attitudes of selfishness, unconcern, controlling others, judging. But, bad as these things are — and all of us need seriously to consider here the place of sacramental penance — they are not the basic orientation of our lives. By far the vast majority of people are not seriously malicious or evil-minded. They do not set out to hurt others in any serious way. Most people have a fundamental will to love God and love their fellow man, and many of them need to be rescued from a certain amount of false guilt.

Without minimizing sin or danger, the new emphasis stresses the presence and power of Jesus as *victorious* over all evil, *in charge* of the world. It sees human persons — for all their sinfulness and limitations — as touched by God with a glorious challenge to freedom and responsibility, to growth and openness. It is a morality centered on real, flesh-and-blood persons, not abstractions.

It is our utter conviction that by far the vast majority of persons are good and try to live responsibly. Because of this conviction we can spend more effort in encouraging people to accentuate the positive than in warning or even mistrusting them. We will catch more flies with honey than with vinegar. Sin is real and powerful, the deadliest thing in the universe; but Jesus is more real and more powerful, and his business is *life*.

Do the Best You Can

We begin as saplings and become trees by a mysterious process of growth that can't be measured every day. The apple tree results from its previous habits of "doing a little bit every day."

What do we say to a friend who's discouraged or confused in the face of a very demanding situation? "Don't worry about it! Do what you can." That's equivalent to saying, "Do the best you can. God doesn't expect any more of anybody."

Our best will never be perfect. It will always reflect our sinful condition. But it ought also to reflect our condition of *being-redeemed*. We are not floating about in the pool of life trying to make it on our own. We are *being* healed and empowered by

Christ. As a popular banner has it, "Please be patient — God isn't finished with me yet." There is something of evil and failure in our best behavior. There is something of good and grace in our worst. The point is, God only deals in *now*. What he may ask us next week, what he asked us to do last week, is not our concern. It's what he wants *now*. And what he wants now is that we positively try to use our head (i.e., our conscience) to do what we can under the present circumstances.

Ripples on the Surface — and the Deep Current

Life is not neat and orderly, like pictures in *Good Housekeeping*. Ask any mother or father, if you haven't entered that noble vocation. "Future shock" seems to be revealing more loose ends every day. It is simply not crystal clear what we ought to do to accentuate the positive in many situations. We may know all the rules and all the prohibitions. But how, precisely, do you love your wife or husband here and now (just not committing adultery is pretty minimal)? What do you say or not say? When? How?

Conscience is simply our attempt to make the decision that the present situation calls for. Obviously this means that we are risking making "mistakes." Not *moral* mistakes, but judgments that had we known more, would have gone in a different direction.

The overriding consideration is our attitude, our deep disposition, our overall orientation, our Gospel spirit. As long as a person is *striving* to accentuate the positive, he will in the long run be growing as a person, in freedom, responsibility and real love.

Confidence in Conscience

Michael Joseph Armbruster didn't see the ridiculousness of "running away" and still coming home for meals, just as his immature cousin Alice may not see the contradiction between being supposedly on her own in marriage and yet running home to mother (by phone at least) for her decisions.

If we are to be mature Christians, we are to be that way all the time, in all decisions. All life is religious and moral. There's no such thing as "mere" business life, social life, artistic life, sex life, diet life, academic life, etc. But for some reason or another we tend to separate our lives into compartments. Some we can handle. For others we have to go to someone for an "answer." It's like calling the police for every fifth argument.

Many people — adults, married, businessmen, teachers, housewives — make many serious and complicated decisions every day. These judgments are *moral,* and have moral implications: e.g., the decision to buy a house somewhere, to invest in a color TV, to join a club, to get married, to vote. Yet, when it comes to something that has a "religious" label on it, the same people feel the need to call a priest and get an absolute "answer," for instance, about marital difficulties, dealing with teenagers, training children, deciding about Sunday Mass, reading a book or having an operation.

Now, we all need someone to listen to us, encourage us, sympathize, help us clarify our thoughts, understand us. And certainly priests can be very helpful. The point is, these people are not seeing their lives *as a whole.* They don't seem to realize that they have the *ability* to judge in these matters just as they are already doing in many other areas in their lives. They are already making serious and complex moral decisions. They should be making the same efforts, going through the same process, in grappling with these "moral" problems. They are not basically different from the *other* moral problems of their life.

God gives us all a conscience to deal with our whole life; that is, he gives us the ability to understand situations, examine all aspects and ramifications, search out alternatives, foresee results and then *choose* the course of action that seems best for all concerned. It is sad that so many Catholics feel that there are some areas of their lives where only a priest can give them an "answer." The priest can and should be a source of information, inspiration and understanding. But he cannot and dare not give "answers" to people as far as their own responsible decisions are concerned. He cannot stand in anyone's shoes. He cannot "read" the situation, the concrete situation, like the one actually involved in it. He cannot fully know the sinfulness, the potential or the experience of another person. He knows general rules and principles. He knows the values involved. He may even be expert in showing people how to search for and arrive at moral decisions. But decision is personal or it is not decision. All my decisions must be *mine*. I cannot let somebody else take my responsibility; I cannot hide behind others, blame them, or give them the "credit" for my life. As the Man of La Mancha said, "I am I, Don Quixote!"

Between the Devil and the Deep Blue Sea

Sometimes we find ourselves in conflict situations. We are "caught." We have to make a decision, and both alternatives promise to have some evil results. Some value or law will get pinched, whatever we decide.

For example, a businessman is faced with giving kickbacks, and thus dealing deceitfully with his associates, or going out of business. A lawyer is faced with ducking his duty or defending a criminal whom he knows to be guilty. A married couple clearly cannot support another child and are convinced they are not strong enough to abstain or practice rhythm.

In many such situations, people are faced with painful alternatives, none of which is certainly and purely good. The rules, the laws, the general principles may be very clear. The problem is that one law is in conflict with another, one value against another, or the person simply cannot "put it all together." No matter what the decision, evil will result. So one is "forced" to compromise by the total situation, by his inability to find a "pure" solution, and by the necessity to do *something.*

So he does the best he can. He chooses that alternative which before God offers the greater hope for good, avoids the greater evil.

In past moral emphasis, which stressed the individual *action,* it was all or nothing. There was an assumption that no *real* moral conflicts were possible, hence no compromise was possible. Whatever we did was black or white, "good" or "evil."

This approach does not match our experience, which does unmistakably tell us that we are often in real conflict situations. Life is not black and white. It is mostly gray, and messy, and loose-ended. Moral decisions do not come easily, and at times they are painfully difficult, and there is *no one way* of acting that is obviously and absolutely the right one.

But we must choose. "Not to decide is to decide." To refuse to choose is itself a choice, for which we are responsible.

Therefore it is important that in our whole life, in our basic orientation, we always try to "accentuate the positive," do the best we can. Out of a positive sincere desire to please God in our whole life, we will in the long run bring the best attitude to individual choices, no matter how perplexing.

Chapter VI

LED BY THE SPIRIT

Wind can blow down a skyscraper or caress a baby's cheek. It can drive flame through a metropolis or keep the tiniest campfire burning. Even though we have scientific meteorologists and weathermen, it is still true that we "do not know where it comes from or where it goes."

Mysterious wind, all-present air, life-giving breath. Scarcely realizing it, we are kept alive by our breathing. With perhaps still less awareness, we are kept alive by the Spirit.

The Spirit came "last" in the account of our salvation — the thunderous wind, the flames of Pentecost. So in our path to the Ten Commandments, we come to the final and most important consideration: life in Christ is possible only by the power of the Spirit.

We have seen that God calls us as persons, not 50,000 dots. We are called to be and to live like our

Father, as sons and daughters who show the family resemblance.

The call we have is sheer gift. Theoretically, God could have created a different kind of world. We can't even imagine what "we" would have been in that world, because in fact our whole experience has been one of being welcomed into this world of God's life.

In other words, God has so arranged it that, whereas he has his way *absolutely* with stars and violets, rivers and rabbits, his way with man is that it must be partly man's way. Things are not the way God wants them unless *we* want them that way; that is, freedom is at the heart of God's design for human life, and the heart of human life is the free response of man.

When he came to man, God decided that man would have to do something about creating himself. That power would be a gift, of course, but it would have to be used by man. As St. Augustine said, "All is from God, but all is from man."

We have seen, also, that we become the person God intends through free and responsible decisions which gradually become one great decision (or basic orientation) about life.

Our response to God must be one of positive and loving freedom. As we have considered, there is a raw freedom that *can* do *anything*. A person who rejects God is aware of the meaning of his actions and sufficiently free in that it is a "cold-blooded" decision, not one induced by ignorance, passion or force. The freedom is real, just as a murderer is real; but it is sterile and self-defeating, as the murderer is, and self-hating and morally suicidal.

To be free, we need freely to accept the power of the Holy Spirit releasing our freedom. Without that power, we can easily become slaves to a counterfeit freedom greedily drinking pleasant poison, whipping about crazily like a firehose that has escaped the fireman's grasp.

The answer we make to God must be a fully personal, human answer, made within our actual human condition. But it cannot be personal unless there is truth and love and freedom. Since only God can create these things and bring them to fulfillment, the "Creator Spirit" is involved.

If anyone loves, if anyone embraces truth, if anyone is free, it is because he shares in the light and power and life of the Spirit.

So we are immersed in a great mystery. We are free, but we are completely in debt to the Spirit for it. Our life decision and decisions are ours; they are also the work of the Spirit of the Father and of Jesus. Thus our answer to God is fully human, and it is also divine: in-Spirited.

We are, therefore — as you would expect of Christians — like Christ. He was a divine person, with a human nature; we are human persons, with a really divine life. If we look closely, we may be surprised at how prominent the Spirit was in Jesus' earthly life. The spirit was the source of his conception by Mary. The Spirit descended upon him at his baptism, and "drove" him into the wilderness where he faced down the devil. He returned "in the power of the Spirit" to Galilee. He was filled with the Spirit. The Spirit, in fact, would be "another"

Paraclete like himself, who would take his place when he went to the Father, and bring them to all truth.

So it is with us. We are put here not just to avoid evil — though we must do that, too, in our own wilderness — but to let the breath of the Holy Spirit fill us as persons, make us ever more like Christ, more aware of God's truth, more loving, more freely decisive and willing to grow. Whatever is not of the Spirit is sin; whatever is of the Spirit is divine life.

But not everything that occurs to our mind is of the Holy Spirit. There is always need to "discern the Spirit," test all things. Many of the aspects of moral theology that came to us through the catechism were actually ways of "discerning the Spirit." Scripture, the liturgy, the teaching of the Church, the rules of conscience and of prudence, the teaching about "actual" grace, i.e., God's (the Spirit's) helping us to act in his life — in these and other ways we were taught to be open and docile to the Spirit (perhaps without having it put in those terms).

Today there is emphasis on the need to be more explicitly aware of the absolute need of the Holy Spirit in our lives.

We are, in this as in other matters, asked to see the wholeness of our lives. Our actions are not isolated and discontinuous elements. They form one basic decision. We are to be responsive and open to the spirit in *all* the aspects of our life.

The shift in emphasis from nature to person, which we have examined, and the consequent em-

phasis on freedom and responsibility have also led to a difference in our notion of what it means to be "led by the Spirit."

Law and/or Love?

Our understanding of "being led by the Spirit" is different today because there is a greater emphasis on love and less on law. The Gospel makes love the primary commandment. Absolutely everything in life has meaning only in relation to love of God, others and oneself.

But this also makes it more difficult to know what "God's will" is in the concrete, since the command to love is so open-ended.

The "law" of the Gospel is very clear, in a way: love your neighbor. The person and example of Jesus are very real and challenging. The Gospel helps us discover aspects of love — respect, mercy, patience, kindness, justice, etc. It even spells out some contradictions to love — pride, selfishness, injustice, unchastity, idolatry. But with all this help, we are left with no "answers" to concrete problems. How, for instance, do you love the people who sell their houses when unwanted persons move into the neighborhood, creating a panic situation in which your own property will lose value? How do you respect your talented boss when you know what he's doing to another worker? What do you say to your godchild who's now living with a boy in a college dorm? What should you do or not do, say or not say, here and now? You must decide. No one can do it for you. Laws, rules, advice, Church teaching, Gospel, may give help, may show general boundary lines, but no one can tell you precisely what to do. Yet the Spirit is prompting you to love and thus to "do God's will." And the prudent decision that is made *is* God's will.

To repeat: "God's will" is not a five-million-page book typed out from eternity, waiting for us to discover — say, by finding line 34 on page 15,673, exactly what we ought to do about Cesar Chavez, the fifth-grade teacher, or the teenagers who ran through your flower bed.

Rather, "doing God's will," i.e., being led by his Spirit, is quite different. It sees God as saying to us, "I've given you life. *Live.* I've given you intelligence, freedom, emotions, imagination, memory. *Use* them. I've given you the whole of creation and history. I've given you Jesus, brothers and sisters, Church, history, creation and my Spirit. You have all you 'need.' Now I want *your* personal response, not somebody else's. I don't have it all figured out for you, like a rat maze that has only one path to the exit. Please me. Surprise me. Be *yourself.*"

Laws are necessary, like the boundaries of a basketball court or the guardrails of a race track. But what's important is what *people* decide to do in the game and the race. Laws are helpful, like signs that say driving over 35 is unsafe on a certain curve in the road. But only people can enjoy driving a car.

The Spirit leads us with his power, with the light of Jesus' revelation, but it is our life to live. He leads us always in the direction of more deep-rooted conversion, more nearly total faith, more generous love; to richer fruitfulness, more selfless service, greater hope and trust in the mercy and power of God.

Being led by the Spirit "drives" us, as it did Jesus, toward the attitude expressed in the Beatitudes — at once very "general" and yet quite distinctive. The Spirit leads us to be ever more poor in spirit, aware of our littleness before God, really hungry for God's holiness, compassionate and forgiving, single-minded and wholehearted, willing to pay the price of being one who reconciles and makes peace, patient and even joyful in suffering and persecution. If we are letting ourselves be led in this direction, we are doing God's will because the Spirit is guiding us.

St. Paul spelled it out. If you want to know the opposite of being led by the Spirit, here's the "fruit" man produces when he rejects the Spirit: lewd conduct, impurity, licentiousness, idolatry, sorcery, hostilities, bickering, jealousy, outbursts of rage, selfish rivalries, dissensions, factions, envy, drunkenness, orgies and the like (Galatians 5,19).

In contrast (and, be it noted, in *general*) the fruit of the Spirit is love, joy, peace — patient endurance, kindness, generosity — faith, mildness, chastity (Gal. 5,22). When we are trying to have and express these attitudes, we are being led by the Spirit.

But what the Spirit leads us to is a seeking and searching within our own hearts and in our own concrete situations. We believe in his abiding presence, but we have to use our own intelligence to consider our situation, discover what is involved, weigh various alternatives, and finally decide on a course of action that we sincerely think is right. In the end we must decide and embody in concrete behavior what we think is the more loving thing. That is what God wants, and all he wants.

In the first half of this book we have attempted to describe the kind of person each of us is called to be: one who is both "keeper" and "fruit" of God's Commandments. He or she is a person being made into the likeness of Christ, a unique individual willing to grow in freedom and responsibility, open and docile to the leading of the Spirit, gradually maturing to a deeper basic orientation of life, patient with the obscurity and risk of particular decisions, always partially weak, selfish and sinful, yet basically trusting and joyful within a Father's care.

In the second half of the book we see this kind of person enriching his or her life with the values *God* has embodied in his Commandments.

Part Two:
WHY JESUS GIVES US HIS COMMANDMENTS

many people are very distressed that children no longer seem to know the Commandments, because they may not be able to recite them from memory. The assumption seems to be that all morality is summed up in the Commandments. There is the further assumption that if you know the Commandments by heart, everything will be fine. This is simply not true. The Commandments do not sum up all morality. They are negative. They prohibit certain actions which are incompatible with Christian living, but they do not indicate what we are to *do,* how we are to live. They spell out some of the ways that certainly are *not* loving, but they do not tell us what to *do* if we are to love God and neighbor, particularly in the concrete.

What is more, it does little good to be able to recite the Commandments if we don't know what they *mean.* We can kill a man in cold blood and we can kill a man in self-defense. We can deliberately deceive someone, and we can justifiably conceal a secret. Unless we know what the Commandments really mean, the values God is promoting and protecting, we cannot observe them.

The Commandments are considered, in the Catholic tradition, expressions of the natural law formulated in the context and historical situation of the Old Covenant. We cannot rightly understand the Ten Commandments in the New Covenant unless we understand them in the light of Christ, and his new commandment of love.

With all this in mind, there is reason to believe that children today may actually be learning *more* about Christian morality than in the past, in a way that is much more positive and balanced. Their lives may be more moral and more fruitful than ours in the long run. Before we condemn the way morality is being taught, we ought to consider the rationale with open minds.

After all, there is also in our past Catholic tradition a method of presenting morality not in terms of commandments, but in terms of virtues, as we today teach it in terms of Christian *values*. One very obvious deficiency in a commandment-morality is that it is very negative. We can, for instance, quickly learn that masturbation, fornication, adultery, homosexuality and a host of other actions are against the Sixth Commandment. But we may not have the faintest idea what chastity or purity *is*. We know what not to do. But what is the positive attitude of a chaste Christian? Why is it valuable to be chaste? What values are damaged or destroyed by impurity?

In a negative emphasis, the implication is that virtue is not a plus but a zero, the absence of certain forbidden actions. No wonder "virtue" has so little appeal! No wonder, too, why parents have so much difficulty answering the questions of their teenagers. Unless a person has some positive knowledge and appreciation of the value of premarital chastity, the prohibition of premarital intercourse will not seem too important.

In this section we propose to set forth briefly how the basic dimensions of Part I carry through in the Ten Commandments, especially in the basic values underlying them: *worship, life, sexuality, justice, truth.* By dealing with one or two concrete moral issues in each of these areas, we hope to show how the Commandments are to be understood and lived in the New Covenant, and in the light of a new approach to morality.

Chapter VII

WORSHIP in Spirit and in Truth

the first three Commandments have to do with our direct personal relationship to God, expressed by our free exercise of the *virtue* of religion.

There is no real religion without love. We are simply distorting the truth if we say that the "God of the Old Testament" was a God of stern and almost cold-hearted judgment, ruling a people whose greatest virtue was fear. It is clear that the Old Testament relationship between God and man was a loving one. The God of the Covenant is a faithful and merciful God, eager for the faithful, loving response of his people, a response that was concretized especially in sacrifice and observance of the law. In the course of time sacrifice and observance of the law lost their inner meaning — gift of self to God, worship.

In the New Covenant, we are called to be sons and daughters of God in Jesus, living totally for the

Father and loving our neighbor as Jesus loves us. Now worship must be, as Jesus said, "in spirit and in truth," as contrasted with that which rested primarily on observance of law. Religion is seen to involve not only formalized acts directed to God, but justice and compassion to our fellowmen. Now the stress is on the fact that in following Jesus we are called to a life that is truly worshipful, religious, *in all its aspects.* As the *Catechetical Directory* says, worship "includes a resolve to fulfill his will in every field of activity, and faithfully to increase in charity the talents given by the Lord" (No. 47).

If we see the first three Commandments in the light of the New Covenant, it is impossible to separate religion and morality and life. All our behavior flows from the basic orientation of our life to God, which expresses itself dynamically in faith, hope and charity directed in Jesus to the Father and always bearing fruit in our relationships with others.

There are, of course, moments in our life when the religious dimension is intensified and becomes more conscious; for instance, when we pray, become particularly aware of God's presence, celebrate the Eucharist. These are moments of *more explicit* faith when we (individually or communally) express ourselves directly: praising God's goodness, begging his forgiveness, offering ourselves (sacrifice), promising something special (vow).

These explicit and conscious times and externals of worship are necessary because we are men and women, not angels. Our prayer is not merely "spiritual" but human, expressed in bodily form. We are not merely individuals, but social beings, members of communities, members of a visible Body called the Church.

What needs to be stressed is that we cannot *limit* worship to these moments. As the Gospel clearly indicates, love of God and love of neighbor are inseparably entwined. St. John expressed this fact most sharply: "If anyone says that he loves God, whom he cannot see, and hates his brother, whom he can see, that man is a liar" (1 John 4,20). To think that worship can somehow be "something by itself" and not inextricably connected with our love of neighbor is to miss the heart of true religion. St. James said, "Looking after orphans and widows in their distress, and keeping oneself unspotted from the world, make for pure worship before our God and Father" (James 1,27).

God wants our whole life — yet by far the greatest part of our life is lived without explicit awareness of the presence of God. This cannot mean that only certain parts of our life are religious, and the rest "neutral" or even bad. The older morality, which tended to see our lives impersonally and in terms of individual acts, lent itself to the feeling that religion and life were separate. The newer morality, with its stress on person and life-orientation, is better able to see life and religion as one whole. The older morality tended to limit "religion" drastically by its stress on obedience to laws and its preoccupation with what was forbidden. The newer morality, emphasizing response to God's call, and stressing what we are to *do*, sees religion as permeating all life.

This can be illustrated by a closer look at two aspects of our "life-expression" of religion: prayer and Mass.

Prayer

We have sometimes seen prayer as an interruption of our "normal" activity; an uninteresting chore to be "gotten in," like emptying the sweeper bag or putting up storm windows.

The mistake was (if we made it) seeing prayer as something *added* to our life, like "Two pills now, then one every six hours." The addition was to be made especially in times of suffering or temptation.

Implicit was the false notion of stopping what we felt was our "real" life. The bell rang for prayer, and our usual activity had to stop. (This led, incidentally, to a completely inhuman notion of "distractions." The rest of life had to be kept out of this isolation cell called "prayer.")

All this made it quite difficult to take St. Paul seriously when he simply said, "Pray always." How could anyone do that?

Second, we sometimes approached prayer as if it were something static. It was not something in which you invested imagination or creativity. You just prayed. Points A, B, C and conclusion. Decades one, two, three. Ten minutes, a half hour. There was a process to go through, and it stayed more or less the same.

This is not to say that prayer was not an expression of deep faith and love, or that it was not part of a life of union with Christ. It's that prayer seemed to require such effort, even heroism. It was a "problem." Out of a deep sense of duty and/or faith we might spend time praying day after day, year after year, but it was far more laborious than it might have been.

To see prayer as something more than an "additive" in our lives is to admit the possibility that God wants something richer, more satisfying and creative.

This means that prayer must be understood in a radically different way, *as an ingredient of all life.* The burden of this book thus far has been that all life is moral and religious, and directed to Jesus. We are responsible and called by God in everything we do. Personal and community growth goes on all the time, not just in prayerful moments. Hence prayer must be something that permeates our whole life.

We believe that this radical nature of prayer means that it is the believer's *search for meaning and direction* — a search that is enlightened and empowered by God's Spirit and leads through man back to God. To be human is to search for meaning, purpose, direction in life. To be Christian is to believe that these values are discovered perfectly in Jesus, and therefore to seek them in him.

Prayer as search for meaning and direction in Christ has three presuppositions.

First, an *incarnational* view of life. Holiness is in this bodily life which God himself shared. It is not in some other "spiritual" world that is presumably divorced from the unwholesome realities of body, world, time and space. God in Christ can be discovered and responded to in the human. God is present in human situations.

Second, God is present in *all* human life and all human situations. Prayer is as wide and as deep as life itself. There are no neutral moments when prayer has to be postponed.

Third, prayer, like life, is *dynamic*. It is bound up with growth and development, and therefore with change. It is part of maturing, an ongoing and never-ending process.

In the dynamic, totally human area, God draws man to search for meaning and direction in Christ.

The meaning sought is an ever-deepening one. Prayer is the experience of ongoing discovery. In prayer we realize "who we are." Some people are irritated by that phrase, as if it should be perfectly obvious who anybody is. He's John Smith, aged 34, married, with three children, plumber, member of the St. Boniface Men's Society, Knight of Columbus, Republican, shoots in the high 80's and is allergic to penicillin. *That's* who he is.

Mrs. Smith knows better. She knows a deeper John Smith. And John Smith should know himself even better. Who is he? He's a person whose actions are filled with God's gracious love, a member of Christ's Body, a witness to the ongoing work of Christ's saving activity in the world, a being in whom the Spirit of God lives, a mysterious person who will live forever. *"Who* am I?" means "Who is the person God is calling me to be?" Prayer then releases an awareness of my own dignity, potential, responsibility and decisiveness in fulfilling these qualities.

Once a man knows that there is a deeper *who* in himself than the statistics show, he sees all other beings in a new light, and prayer is a search for the deeper meaning of all men and women.

Prayer, therefore, makes us questioners. What's really going on here? What's the meaning beneath the surface? Why did I react in this way? How should I respond? Why do I feel so good, or so insecure, or suspicious? Why was I gentle or harsh or silent? What does it all *mean*?

Because all roads through men's hearts lead to the One who is true and good, prayer becomes a search for the meaning of "who" God is. It becomes a heartfelt experience of the wonder of the relationship between God and you and me.

Pilgrims, Not Wanderers

Prayer is a search for direction. We are aware that God is present and is calling us to go in a certain direction, like Abraham; to *follow* Christ; to *come* to him. To take steps, to follow a path, to have a goal and to take purposeful steps toward it.

Here the questions are: What am I called to become? Where do I go from here? How do I act in this situation? How do I observe this law, carrying out this belief of the Church? How do I respond to my neighbors' experiences of injustice, poverty, oppression? How should I be responding to my wife or husband, my children, my boss, my class, my teacher, in the present situation? Where will I go on vacation? Where is my whole life going? Where should it be going?

There are no pat answers in a divine computer,

released by saying six Our Fathers and six Hail Marys. The Gospel is something to be lived, not diagrammed. God's will is that I make up my mind in his light and with his power. He calls me to grow by giving and receiving, questioning and deciding, willing to take the risks of serving God and to pay the cost.

So we are back to prayer as an ingredient of all life. God calls me in all my human situations, i.e., in all situations. Some experiences of life are apparently meaningless, if not absurd; a loved one's death, whether sudden or slow; loss, betrayal, failure. But to the degree that we are in conscious relationship with a loving Father through Christ, *we* are not meaningless. Faith sees life as a whole — a gradual growth of intimacy with God. All the ugly, painful, crushing things that happen to us *can* draw out of us totally "meaningful" responses of courage, trust, even greater freedom in guiding the course of our own lives in faith. There are no "unprayerful" times if we are always searching for meaning and direction with a consciousness of God's loving Spirit being with us.

We need to reassure ourselves that the search can take an endless number of forms, according to the creative spirit we bring to it. Thus, reading a book, watching a movie, conversing, listening to a lecture, swimming, dancing, sitting in silent wonder at a sunset, taking part in a demonstration, shopping — all can be prayer. And not only *can* be. What good reason is there to say they are not?

On the other hand, we often have no choice but to adapt ourselves to the limitations or demands of the situation. There are times when we need to be alone to pray in an intense way. At other times we need the support and inspiration of others, especially close friends, or our family, or community. Some moments — perhaps rare ones — may be filled with ecstasy: unexpectedly at the Eucharist, or alone at night on the lake shore, or in a moment of deep sharing with a loved one.

And there are other times when there is nothing but the dark night, Gethsemani, or the desert wandering in faith. But perhaps the greatest prayer Christ lived was in Gethsemani.

It is only *within* this ongoing search and alertness for God that we can see the value and necessity of particular "times" of prayer. Within our whole life of prayer there will be highlight times of special concentration and intensity.

It would be foolhardy to suggest that we no longer need actual times, even regular times of prayer during the day. Perhaps the same confusion has arisen here as in other discussions: in the emphasis on *overall* meaning and value, there may seem to be a de-emphasis on *particular* actions and practices. The fact is, of course, that one is impossible without the other. The "prayer of our whole life" needs the concentration and even the discipline of particular times of praying. Actual times of prayer need the momentum and totalness of life to have something to express.

The search for meaning and direction will involve a growing understanding and acceptance of oneself, of God, of others, and a growing effectiveness in responding. Under the guidance of the

Holy Spirit, it will result in greater self-awareness, self-possession, self-expression and greater self-transcendence.

Even in pain and suffering, confusion and uncertainty, we will experience a growing sense of the kind of peace only Christ can give, a deep wonder at the mystery, harmony and beauty of life.

This is growth, personal maturing as a human person, a believer, a member of Christ. We will gradually experience a great sense of being authentic, faithful, consistent. We will sense both fullness and fruitfulness in lives of service.

This is worship of God in spirit and in truth.

The Mass

Pity the poor high school religion teacher. He or she, layman, nun or priest, is one of the most badly quoted and unfairly "attacked" public figures in the Church today. They should be getting the grateful appreciation of parents for being willing to help kids actually wrestle with the complex moral problems of today's world, a task that is terribly challenging, often frustrating, sometimes apparently futile. Instead, teachers are getting the blame for supposedly telling the kids that "you don't have to go to Mass on Sunday if you don't want to."

On the face of it, parents should realize that at the worst there couldn't be that many teachers saying it so badly. Why then, has this sentence spread like wildfire from coast to coast among Catholic teenagers?

The teenagers say something far deeper is in-

volved, something that has to be worked out before their parents lose their minds worrying about getting their bodies inside a church building for 37 minutes each Sunday morning.

The young are telling their elders, "Mom, Dad, we hope you are going to Mass on Sunday *because you want to*." Not merely because you think it's a mortal sin if you don't. Not only because you have to. We need something to hope for. There doesn't seem to be anything in the world that anybody really believes in, except making money. Show us there's really some meaning to being a Christian.

It's no wonder that some parents are *saying* the wrong reasons *for* going to Mass on Sunday (even though deep in their hearts they may have the right reasons and can't express them).

They are speaking out of a culture and catechism that was peculiarly preoccupied with mathematics. Here's a quote (from a once-highly-regarded moral theologian) about *how much* of the Mass had to be missed before one committed a venial or mortal sin: "The omission of a small part of the Mass is a venial sin: from the beginning until after the Credo or up to the offertory; everything after Communion; everything up to the epistle plus everything after Communion; the preface alone.

"It would be a serious sin to omit a notable part of the Mass — for instance, from the beginning until after the offertory; everything up to the Gospel and all that follows Communion; from the preface to the consecration; from the consecration to the Our Father; the consecration or the Communion themselves, even if one were present in between; the consecration alone."

There was even a discussion of whether one fulfilled the precept by hearing two half-Masses.

In fairness, we should also say that the older theologians emphasized the need for full realization, full freedom. But we got off the track — perhaps it was the externals-oriented culture we lived in — by being mathematical, preoccupied with *what* instead of *why*.

It's as though a husband would ask, "How many nights do I *have* to be home with my wife?" Or a wife, "Do I fulfill my wifely obligation by staying at dinner until the dessert?"

A good friend of mine says she is tired of being told she's asking the "wrong questions."

But these *are* the wrong questions, so the answers don't help. If husbands and wives start asking questions like that, they've got far deeper troubles. And so it is with the whole wrangle about Sunday Mass.

Sometimes, of course, the "wrong" questions are merely surface expressions. Most families sound at times like a group of strangers. If all we heard of Joe Smith's family were some Sunday morning hassles ("Why do I have to go to Mass?" "Because I said so, that's why!") we might suspect iron-bound authoritarianism and externalism. But most parents feel that young people want somebody to show them standards and discipline to support them in their challenging exploration of a free and responsible life. The sometimes gruff "We're all going to Mass because that's what we do in this family!" can be either reassuring or repelling, depending on whether or not a deep and loving relationship exists in the family. So again, we're at the thesis of the new morality: the individual act is important, but it must be seen in terms of the whole picture.

As we have seen, the newer emphasis in moral theology is on personal faith, on freedom in giving generous response to God and man, on accepting inner responsibility for life, on love and community as the most basic values of Christianity. This fits hand in glove with the new awareness of the values in Scripture and liturgy.

The heart of the matter is this: God has entered into a new covenant with us, and presumably we have entered the same covenant with him, accepting his offer freely and gratefully. This means that our Father brings together a loving community in Jesus, so that all the members can be healed and enabled to live a fully human and even divine life. This life is seen as entering into Christ, living on the power of the Spirit he sends us, seeing life in the light of his Gospel.

The most perfect expression of this life *should be* the Mass. Everything comes together and culminates here — the living Christ gathering us around the one altar; the community of loving and forgiving brothers and sisters; the saving embrace of God; the nourishing of the Bread of life; the joyful worship given to the Father; the celebration of divine life; the going forth to witness with courage and peace.

The Mass is a statement-in-action about our whole life. It comes out of an awareness of what our vocation is, as Christians: to grow in our baptismal covenant, to mature towards being like Christ; to enter into his death and resurrection, both as individuals and as community.

Mass says that all the ups and downs of life, the drudgery and pain, delight, the blank moments, the tragedy and comedy — all the pieces of the jigsaw puzzle — are the way we continue the saving work of Christ today. And all these things are part of the human-divine offering we make with him in the Mass. They are all caught up in the celebration of God's loving and healing power as it comes to us in his human-divine Son, our brother and priest.

The Mass is the Christian community being moved by a total vision of life to come together and say, "There *is* Good News. Life does make sense. There is hope, and healing and power to be good and happy. It is a public statement of faith."

As the Council says, the Mass is the expression of something that's already in the community and in individuals — a sense of personal value before God, an awareness of being called to something strong and beautiful, a responsibility to let God's power flow through life, and a sense of responsibility to others — not just to help them, but to be helped by them, to give and receive, to love and be loved — to *be* the body of Christ in a visible way.

The very expression of this faith is a stimulus to faith. We go to Mass because we have something to express; having expressed it, we have a deeper awareness of why we came.

God himself has compared his relationship to us to that of husband and wife. If there is love between husband and wife, their celebrations, meals, conversation, silence, working together are expressions of one single central fact of life: they love each other. Difficulties, problems, sins, yes — but the deep central current sustains and washes all.

So it is with Mass and religion and faith. Mass is an expression of an already existing love and commitment, a sense of privilege in belonging to the Body of Christ, a desire to express love of God, love of man and — yes, the third part of the commandment — a sense of loving and affirming myself because God has given me great value and dignity by taking me seriously.

So the question is *not* "Must I go?" or "How often must I go?" or "How big a sin if I miss a part, or all, of Mass?" The most basic question is "*Why* should I go? What does the Eucharist *mean* in my life? What does it mean to *me*? How do I grow in understanding and appreciating its meaning for me? How do I live its meaning in my daily life?"

If I have positive answers to these questions, I begin to understand why someone would feel he *ought* to attend Mass every Sunday and also to *want* to participate in this most significant and important celebration, whether there is a law or not.

Hence it seems quite evident that if people, especially young people, are not going to Mass, the reason most likely is not because they are "bad" people, or are rebellious and disobedient. The reason is much more likely to be found elsewhere: in a lack of understanding of the Christian vocation, in *not yet* realizing what it means to be a free and also responsible member of a community or what faith-

and-sacrament have to say about the totality of life. In other words: immaturity, lack of knowledge, lack of understanding — problems that beset maturing people all their lives.

There is no "magic" in attending Mass. The fact that many who attend Mass regularly and yet live in a way that is very un-Christian testifies to this. Because there is no "magic" in attending Mass, there appears little or no reason to drag someone into church. Some tend to think that by forcing young (or old) people to go to Mass often enough, they will come to like it or appreciate it. This is not only untrue, it may be one of the best ways of defeating the very purpose of the law requiring attendance at Sunday Mass. Why do so many Catholic school children who attended Mass *daily* for 12 years stop completely when they enter college? The law requiring Sunday Mass was intended to embody the value of the Eucharist in Christian life. If that value is not gradually perceived and appreciated personally, the law serves no purpose for that person.

Moreover, we often fail to appreciate the law of personal growth. Teenagers necessarily go through a process of interiorizing the values they will live by, including fundamental faith values. This takes time. It involves ups and downs, trial and error. There seems little value in unnecessarily "pushing" them or trying to hurry up this process. They must be given time to grow and mature as Christians. They need trust and encouragement. By the grace of God and their sincere response, they will grow. If in the process they attend Mass irregularly or not at all, the first question is: What does this represent in terms of their growth to maturity? A regression, a mere thoughtless phase, or a wrestling with problems on other and possibly deeper levels of faith? Whatever the demands of discipline, they need from adults the willingness to communicate and be patient, as well as the convincing example of adult convictions.

All of us, young and old, might well ask ourselves what we contribute to the fitting celebration of Sunday Mass. The Three Musketeers were not the only ones who had the slogan, "All for one and one for all." That happens to be the definition of community. From priest to the wallflower in the rear, from lector to the late-comers clattering down the aisle, we might all ask ourselves, "Is this the joyful celebration of a community that really believes that it is the visible gathering of the Body of Christ? What kind of unity are we expressing? Is it any more than the singleness of purpose seen in a crowded bus station? Why are we so self-conscious, unwilling even to smile at the person next to us, much less shake his hand?" We have all been baptized into a sharing of the priesthood of Christ. Do we find our place in church an honor? A burden? We give such an example, and yet blame the young for not wanting to go to Mass!

Finally, people are rightfully distressed when someone says "Missing Mass on Sunday is not a mortal sin." This is just as misleading as to say, "Missing Sunday Mass is always and each time a mortal sin." As Pope Paul has reiterated, participation in Sunday Mass is "more than ever a grave duty." But, as stressed in Part I, it is quite another matter to say that this particular person is guilty of mortal sin in missing Sunday Mass. To assess the personal guilt of missing Sunday Mass we must consider much more than the *fact* of omission. We need to know "why." What is going on in that person's life? What appreciation of the value of Mass does he have? Is he wrestling with other and deeper problems in his life? Only in the light of these personal considerations can we assess personal guilt. Only when we see this "grave duty" of participating in Sunday Mass in the framework of faith, in our whole Christian life, can we have some real sense of its obliging force, some appreciation of the *meaning* of this command, and so be able to fulfill it — or reject it.

In summary, the first three of the Ten Commandments are a somewhat more specific statement of the First Great Commandment. They call us to a full personal and community relationship to God (religion) and to the personal and social expression of that relationship (worship). Our response is a continuous one, brought to intensity and public expression at certain times and places. Religion and life, morality and faith, prayer and worship, permeate our whole life. We are to be Christ-centered and Christ-supported, in the quiet of our room, in community with others and around the altar-table of the new covenant.

Chapter VIII

LIFE: The Gift and the Giving

the Bible begins and ends with praise of life. "The Lord God formed man out of the clay of the ground, and blew into his nostrils the breath of life, and so man became a living being." And at the end of the Book of Revelation: "The grace of the Lord Jesus Christ be with you all! Amen."

Clay, spirit, grace. A holy human trinity that is God's noblest work: a unique human being, totally dependent on God's gift yet independent with the gift of freedom. Not an animal, not an angel, not God. A human person. Alive, breathing, eternal.

Life is so obviously our greatest treasure that we don't even think about gratitude for it. Yet it is not so obvious a good that men will not be tempted to destroy it out of greed, anger or plain stupidity.

Hence it was inevitable that one of the Great Commandments of God should protect the greatest value: human life. "Thou shalt not kill."

Even supposing what never happened, namely that there was such a thing as "mere" human life not destined to see God, the Commandment would still have been basic. But the life that we respect is the life that will rest in God's life forever. It is at the heart of the Good News: "I have come that you may have life, life to the full."

Today, human life is faced with two extreme possibilities. On the one hand, with total destruction. In submarines, on the wings of bombers, deep in the earth, are the cold engines of death, pointed at the heart of other "great" nations, waiting to spew fire and poison on every living being there.

On the other hand, we are on the threshold of unbelievable enrichment. In great hospitals and research centers, men take gigantic strides in diagnosing and curing almost every disease. Even greater breakthroughs are just on the other side of the horizon. Already we know of heart transplants and of the detection of genetic defects.

We are told that genetic surgery, test-tube fertilization, even cloning — the "engineering" of human beings — is on the way.

It is no longer just a question of protecting and preserving life, now it's a matter of controlling and directing human life. It's not just struggling against malnutrition, disease and injury, but of directly intervening to enhance the quality of human life.

This raises a new set of moral questions: Who is going to exercise this control? What guidelines will the "controllers" follow? Who will judge whether or not the intervention is for the improving or the corrupting of human life? What effects will the effort to control life have on the individual person, the family, society?

The all-important aspect of the matter is that in dealing with concrete problems, specific moral issues, we come to them with a *fundamental attitude* that grows out of our experience of God's self-revealing in Christ.

This attitude, or set of convictions, underlies our judgments of moral conduct. Christian prudence seeks to embody this attitude, these convictions in particular instances.

First, then, we look at life in the light of the Gospel and the teaching of the Catholic Church. Then we will treat some of the concrete moral issues in terms of this basic outlook. We hope the values of person, freedom, responsibility and basic orientation will be evident.

1. *Every human life is the creation and gift of God.* Life does not just "happen," it is not an accident. The awesome mystery of life is that we exist because God wills us into existence as persons. We are the children of God's love more completely than the most "wanted" baby ever begotten by man.

Obviously God "depends" on human parents for both the procreation and education of human persons. The use as well as the abuse of persons affects both these activities. A child can be conceived in beautiful and unselfish love as well as in selfishness and unconcern. A child, once born, can become a real "somebody" in his own mind through the love of his parents, or he can be paralyzed into self-doubt by his obvious unwelcomeness.

But, though God "submits" to human freedom in all that can be done to a human being "from the outside," there is something about every human being that is God's own creation and concern. Persons come only from his creative power, no matter by what crooked or pleasant human paths.

God says the same thing about procreation and birth that he says about all life: "I call persons to myself within the circumstances of everyday life. I ask for responsibility, courage, faith and love in all these circumstances. If they are lacking in those who procreate and educate, the human person they destroy or damage is still *my* precious child, and I will give it the grace to be with me forever in spite of the cruel circumstances into which it is forced."

Catholic faith has the absolute conviction that there is no creation of God so precious and noble as a human being, precisely because unlike all other creatures man is made in the image of God and called to share his own life eternally. Every human being is taken seriously by God. We are not only privileged to be created by God, we have the dignity of being like God: personal, free, eternal, called to share with Christ the inheritance of a generous Father.

Our never-merely-human life is meant to be fulfilled by grace. "God *chose* us in him before the world began, to be holy and blameless in his sight, to be full of love; he likewise predestined us through Christ Jesus to be his adopted sons. Such was his will and favor" (Eph. 1:4, 5).

At the heart of human life, then, is a basic and absolute dependence on God. All life, all living, is a gift. The much abused word "humility" is an expression of this total dependence. God puts our life — our selves — into our hands, but as gift, as his creation, to be cherished and respected with reverence and faith.

The most basic attitude about life, then, is gratitude and total dependence on the good God who created and who creates it. No human being has the ultimate say-so about life — his own or another's. Before any human decision about life, man must listen to the God who gives the gift.

2. *The gift of human life is in terms of persons.* We cannot talk about human life except by talking about persons. This should be so obvious as to be tautology. Yet some of those who favor abortion argue that the human fetus is "alive" and yet not a person.

This sounds something like the distorted view of "grace" — as something stored in huge containers in heaven, like wine or soap powder. When somebody lacks "some," a portion is scooped out of the container and shipped to the human "container" who needs it.

Life is not of a piece, like a bolt of cloth or an ocean of water. There is no human life except in this person — this unique, unsharable, free, eternal, uncopiable, wonderful individual called Joe or Mary or Wanda Sue.

Persons exist only in life as it is, in endless variations of development, moral success or failure, physical health or sickness, pleasant or frustrating circumstances. It is of the very nature of being a person that we are always potentially better or worse, on the way forward or backward.

Yet the fact that a person has not reached a certain level of development has no bearing whatsoever on his or her dignity and value as a person. The child just beginning life in the womb, the one-year-old baby, the adolescent, the adult man or woman, the feeble octogenarian — are in varying stages of growth — or, in the last instance, of physical decline. Many factors can impede growth — brain damage, blindness, psychological trauma.

But beneath it all, we recognize one supremely valuable fact. God takes every person seriously. He addresses each person with a personal call. He wills the eternal happiness of every unique human being, and what he wills, he carries out effectively. Nothing that accident or malice can do to a human person can prevent God from having his way: a personal relationship with us that involves freedom and mature loving response.

In many cases we do not know how this happens, but we know that it does. And we respect the mystery of personal life.

3. *Therefore, the gift of our personal life is a call to growth and development.* Human life, even the most contemplative, is on the move. To be alive is to act, go into new situations, have a broader awareness of the meaning of life, love more generously, forgive more willingly, risk more courageously.

On the one hand, biological and psychological aspects of our one person develop and mature, then deteriorate and wane. But as *persons* we are meant to grow continuously throughout our life.

The spirit does not grow old, even if its external expression may be hindered by rheumatism, cancer, emotional pain or external force. As long as consciousness and freedom can operate, every moment is a step toward greater maturity in love or a step backwards toward selfishness and personal retardation.

Respect for this unique gift of personal maturing life, then, will entail the responsibility of promoting personal growth in ourselves and others. It means being concerned that *all circumstances* of anyone's life be conducive to this growth. Respect for human life means deep concern not just for life as against death — as if it were all black and white — but for the *quality* of life.

4. *Since life is personal and growing, it is always in relationship to other people.* Human life is social by nature. Hence respect for life means an awareness of the essential values of family, community, society. I am and express myself by giving and receiving. Paradoxical as it seems, the human person's uniqueness is most evident when he is in relationship with other unique persons. I exist as a real individual in the very midst of a community. I cannot make it on my own unless I make it with others.

This means more than cooperation in getting food, clothing and shelter, building skyscrapers or laying railroad tracks. No one can be true to himself as a person unless he is in a *loving* relationship with others. The most basic fact of a person's life is that he is in the image of God — hence one who must love and be loved in order to be what he is and become what he can become. The capacity to give oneself and receive the gift of others is the essence of personal life, and therefore of the Good News, because it means being like God. That's the way God is. If he creates persons like himself, he doesn't need to "add" laws. It's in our bones that to be persons we must love each other in community.

This is the place to stress that the self-giving that is basic to personal growth involves freedom, self-determination. Loving self-giving must be a free personal choice. It cannot be forced, it cannot be done or decided by someone else. I cannot make your decisions and you cannot make mine.

A question might be raised, here. What about infants, mentally retarded, insane persons? Many factors obviously prevent or impede them from growth as persons. They cannot give themselves in the free and personal way just described. Are they condemned to an inhuman existence?

It is true that external circumstances, accidents or the consequences of others' sinfulness may keep some persons from achieving significant maturity. But two observations are warranted. First, these human persons have a destiny beyond the earthly. They are called to eternal sonship with God in Christ. This remains fully possible within the providence of God for those who cannot achieve full maturity on earth. How the good God takes care of this we do not know. We are sure he does.

Second, we ought not to underestimate the interrelatedness and mutual influence of persons who do not function in obviously personal ways, e.g., the infant, the retarded child, the senile lady living with a family. There is giving and receiving going

on in these families, and it would be greatly over-simplifying to say that persons like those just mentioned are entirely passive, not giving. They may be awakening in other members of the family a far deeper Christian response than if they were in perfect health.

In summary, our attitude toward life holds that human life is a gift from God. It is given to be personal, and with a view to growth in giving oneself unselfishly in relationships with other persons.

From this position, we can now add two further points:

1. *Physical-biological life is not an absolute value,* i.e., it can give way before a greater good. We may give our life to save another from drowning. Defending one's own life may result in the taking of another's life. We may, and we should, give our lives in the sense of spending ourselves in loving service. We may risk our life when there is reasonable hope of achieving a proportionate good for ourselves or others.

But in some sense personal human life is an absolute value. Involving growth through loving, it sums up the very purpose of God's eternal plan and is bound up with our eternal destiny. It is the basic value in which all other human values have their roots. Ultimately, personal life is oriented to self-determination, a decision for or against God himself. Understood in this full sense, human life cannot be rightly subordinated to any other value.

2. *Respect for personal human life obliges us to use all the means and opportunities reasonably available to care for our life and that of others; that is,*

those means and opportunities which offer reasonable hope of preserving or improving life. We must care for our personal life and that of others, protect and improve it, precisely so that we can all grow as persons in so doing.

Respect for another's personal life is completely independent of a consideration of what work or function that person can perform. The life of the most helpless cancer victim, the most senile man, the most retarded child, is as valuable to God as that of the greatest saint, athlete or "producer" in the world.

Respect for personal life means that we live and work, therefore, for the good of all human persons, especially for their freedom to be and to grow as persons.

Some Concrete Issues

We are now able to formulate some principles and consider at least a few of today's moral issues concerning personal life.

First principle: Personal existence from conception to death is the most basic human value. All others presuppose this primary, God-given one. Therefore, no other human value is great enough to justify the *direct* termination of *innocent* human life.

All human persons have a right to life. This right is absolute in the sense that no human person can "own" another human person. No human person can lay claim to the life of another human person so fully as to have power of life or death. No *other* right can supercede the right to life. In this sense, the right to life is absolute.

107

At times we do, and may, take human life. I may be unjustly attacked. I have a right to defend my life, even if in doing so I kill my attacker. Such an attacker does not fulfill the condition of being *innocent*. Likewise a doctor who rushes on a dark, rainy night to deliver a baby might kill a child who runs in front of his car. That would be the termination of innocent life, but it would not be *directly* intended. Our principle speaks of the *direct* termination of *innocent* human life as absolutely immoral.

Note also that the principle holds true whether or not the person is actually capable of conscious human activity at all (e.g., prior to birth) or only in a limited way (e.g., in cases of retardation, mental illness, or senility).

In attempting to formulate this first principle, we are aware of many pressing questions concerning abortion, mercy-killing, elimination of mongoloids, the insane and criminals. We do not intend to treat all these specific issues in a complete way. But some observations must be made.

Concerning abortion: it is gravely immoral to directly intervene to terminate the life of a fetus that cannot live outside the womb by itself. With all due respect for the personal rights of the mother, even in the case where the mother has conceived as a result of criminal attack, that fetal right to life is most basic and should prevail. The right to personal existence and self-determination *includes* the right not to be put out of existence once human conception has occurred. There is a clear genetic evidence that with conception the process of *growth and development has actually begun*. This is true, even though we can't pinpoint clearly and exactly the various stages and aspects of this process. Complicated and still largely unknown as this whole process is, we do have the *incontrovertible fact that no human person ever comes from an unfertilized ovum, or from semen alone.* Every human person develops from a fertilized ovum, and every fertilized ovum that develops becomes a human person.

Concerning euthanasia: direct intervention to terminate the life of mongoloids, the insane, the elderly, those with terminal cancer or intractable pain is gravely immoral. It is the deliberate destruction of human life under the guise of "putting them out of their misery," whether they request it or not.

Persons like these, the intellectual argument runs, are of no *use*; therefore, they are of no *value*. They cannot produce or function. They are declared "waste" by a materialistic society. They are burdensome and expensive. Why not kill them, then, especially if they request a "merciful" end?

On the other hand, there are no doubt sincere people who feel that it is a matter of compassion to release someone from intolerable pain or what is apparently a hopeless existence.

Now that the abortionists have won their battle before the Supreme Court, the mercy-killers will take over the battleground.

To be clear and well-grounded in our discussions, let us re-emphasize one of the essentials of being a person, namely, that it involves being social. Full humanness can come only in human relationships. Hence it is misleading and distorting to evaluate the "worth" of persons apart from this interrelatedness. For example, a six-month-old baby cannot relate positively, or at best in a very minimal way. Others can and do relate humanly and personally to the child and grow in the process. The whole situation is a very human and personal one, and very fruitful for the entire family as well as for the child.

Similarly with the mentally crippled or the senile. They may be unable to actualize their *full* capacity for human, interpersonal relationships. Yet they can be the *focus* of others who can and do relate to them in a way that is good and fruitful for all. So, when the question of euthanasia arises, we need to see it in terms of the interrelatedness of human persons. Such a total human and personal view reveals the inherent value, and this apart from the narrow view of the crippled persons' ability to respond perfectly.

Only God knows what terrible effects would occur in human society if our attitude toward the physically and mentally crippled would prompt us to spend our resources to *eliminate* such people rather than to spend ourselves compassionately caring for them at whatever cost. This giving is most conducive to our growth as persons in society, and so to human life itself. The alternative would be like turning the whole world into a concentration camp!

Second principle: Every human person has the right and the duty to use the ordinary means, resources and opportunities available for preserving and fostering life, health and personal growth.

This implies that no one has the right to deny another such ordinary means: ordinary medical care, operations, medication. On the positive side, this principle obliges all to take reasonable care of health and life and to make reasonable effort to foster personal growth — physically, emotionally, intellectually, spiritually. Such an obligation flows from the value and purpose of human life itself. We must take whatever reasonable steps are necessary to ensure the realization of the goals of personal existence.

But, this principle also implies that there are limits to our efforts to care for health and life. No one has the duty of using extraordinary means to preserve and foster health and life; for example, procedures and treatment that offer no real hope of cure, or which entail excessive or disproportionate difficulty, pain or expense. The distinction between ordinary and extraordinary means becomes crucial in many cases, e.g., for persons with terminal cancer, serious heart impairment, etc.

In concrete cases it can be difficult, even impossible, to discern with certainty when a means is extraordinary. But whenever such a judgment is prudently reached after due deliberation, such means may be foregone, even refused, without disregarding the value of life. On the contrary, the very attitude toward life described above can help in reaching such judgments. Thus, patients in a coma with no hope of recovery can reasonably be presumed to want no extraordinary means used to preserve biological life. Again, a 60-year-old man may legitimately refuse expensive heart surgery, especially when this expense would seriously burden his wife or relatives.

Third principle: The human person has the right to risk or endanger life or health to achieve a proportionate good for himself or others, foreseeing that such a course may result in serious injury to himself or even in death.

"Greater love than this no one has but that he lay down his life for his friends." Thus, a man may risk his life in very bad weather to drive someone seriously ill to the hospital. A person may jump in front of an onrushing car in order to push a child from its path. A soldier may fall upon a grenade lest its explosion kill others. One may agree to have one of his kidneys transplanted into his brother, or to be involved in a serious medical experiment to seek a cure for cancer.

Sometimes, especially in cases of organ transplants and medical experiments, every reasonable precaution must be taken to safeguard freedom of consent, the avoidance of unnecessary risks and the hope of proportionate good. In general, however, it is morally permissible to take such risks for the sake of others.

Persons grow and achieve the purpose of life by free and loving giving of self to and for others. The taking of such risks is in full harmony with human and Christian respect for life.

There are many other moral questions that arise when we consider human life. Some of these questions, particularly those having to do with genetic intervention, cloning, test-tube babies, artificial insemination, are in a way even more serious than those we have touched upon. They concern much more than protecting and preserving human life! They have to do with controlling, directing, improving it. What is more, they involve the very future of the family, of marriage and procreation. The scope of this book does not allow us to go into all these matters. But it should be emphasized that much research and experimentation is already going on in these areas. There are serious moral questions about the research itself and the manner in which it is conducted. Much more serious moral questions deal with how, and by whom, and according to what norms, the fruit of this research will be *used*. The welfare of *human, personal, social* life is at stake as never before. Serious study is urgently needed.

We can be open to all developments which respect personal life while attempting to improve it. We do not act independently of God, who alone can create life, but with faith in his power we work every day to protect and enrich the most valuable of God's creations — the life of human persons.

Chapter IX

SEXUALITY:
The Need and
Power for
Communion

■ n our open and permissive society, many people feel that the Sixth and Ninth Commandments (or the Seventh and Tenth, as listed by Jews and some Protestants) are the most confused and violated area of morality. They wonder "where it will all end." To others, mankind has achieved a breakthrough in sexual knowledge and practice.

The change in attitudes and behavior is profound enough to be called a revolution. Hence, theologians are almost unanimous in urging serious re-examination of the whole area of sexuality. We shall attempt to do this in terms of the new approach described in Part One.

In everyday language the words *sexuality* or *sex* are largely restricted to genital sexuality, man's ability to engage in intercourse or to have sexual experience. In this chapter we are using these words in a much broader sense. Genital sexuality cannot be rightly understood or evaluated except when seen in the light of the person's total sexuality.

To appreciate the goodness and beauty of human sexuality, we begin with some basic and supposedly obvious facts. First, it is God who created us men and women. "Male and female he created them." God is the author of sexuality, "and he saw that it was good."

What is more, God himself was "made flesh," had sexuality. If we didn't catch the goodness from the fact of creation, we certainly can't miss it from the fact that Jesus was and is a fully sexual human male — something for all believers in the Incarnation to ponder.

Fulfilling the work of Christ, the Holy Spirit possesses us in our humanness and therefore our sexuality to enable us, as men and women, to become and live as sons and daughters of the Father. Through God's love the whole human being — therefore, the sexual human being — is offered redemption from sin and its enslaving effects. The whole human being is offered transforming grace to live, die, and rise again as man or woman.

These basic facts must pervade our understanding of Christian vocation and response. It is as men and women that we are called to live in Christ. We are called to respond precisely as *sexual persons* — not in spite of being such.

Sexual morality has been presented in the Catholic Church, particularly by some theologians and preachers, in seriously misleading ways. The deficiencies of moral theology showed up glaringly in this area. So, if moral theology needed to be renewed, as Vatican II said it did, that renewal should show up especially in the area of sexual morality. The deficiencies are quite apparent to most Catholics. Let's recall them briefly.

First, there has been an overemphasis and excessive concern about sexual immorality as compared with other sinfulness. Perhaps it would be more accurate to say there was far too little stress on other more important areas of morality, such as social justice. At any rate, the lack of balance became great and widespread. All too frequently the impression was created that the Sixth and Ninth Commandments were the *only* Commandments, or that sins against these two Commandments were the worst sins. Indeed, the very word "immorality" became so limited as to be almost equivalent to sexual immorality.

Second, some errors of history, springing from Platonism, Manichaeism and Puritanism, saw life as all black and white and put the human body on the "bad" side. This view has infected the attitude of some Catholics towards sexuality. Their feeling is that sex is somehow tainted, unbecoming, "dirty," practically uncontrollable and something to be beaten down at all costs. One of the strange aberrations that stemmed from this was a kind of "angelism." Human beings should live and act like angels, as if they had no bodies, no sexuality.

All this was conducive to a very *negative* attitude. Practically every Catholic asked to describe purity would do so by listing what was forbidden. Hardly anyone seemed to have a positive appreciation of sex. Paradoxically, the very vehemence of the effort to repress sexuality only served the opposite purpose — it became an overwhelming preoccupation. The consequences in terms of false guilt-feelings and distorted judgments of conscience were very serious.

Third, in the past all morality and especially sexual morality was excessively *act-centered*, i.e., focused on the individual external act, objective and "out there." This led to an excessively biological and physiological approach. The physical act or fact became the primary moral consideration. As a result, many young people had a deep and pervasive feeling that there must be some guilt — or at least unwholesomeness — attached to the most normal and even involuntary manifestations of sexuality that occurred to their bodies or minds, e.g., the very presence of sexual fantasy or the very fact of genital sensations. This was due not only to a simplistic notion of the understanding and freedom required for real sin, but also to a lack of awareness of the dynamics of personal growth, not to speak of an ignorance of psychosexual processes.

The root of this deficiency lay in the *static* character of moral theology in general, and its application to sexual morality in particular. The same laws were applied indiscriminately to children, teenagers, adults, to the single and the engaged. It was a matter of "all or nothing." Strangely, while admitting and accepting the fact that no one is perfect and needs to grow in all the other virtues, the impression was clearly given that one was either 100 per cent "pure" or was guilty of sin.

Finally, a great source of distortion in sexual

morality was the almost all-determining stress given to procreation without due regard for other aspects of sexuality. When this is done, it results in a narrow, impersonal, distorted view of sexuality.

The new approach to morality, as we have seen, seeks to place primary stress on the human person, on freedom and responsiblility, and on interrelatedness of persons (community). To put it another way, there is primary stress on the law of love and on the basic moral imperative to grow and develop *as human persons* precisely in and through love for other persons. The new approach, while aware of the powerful presence of sin and disorder in personal and social life, emphasizes that personal growth takes place only *gradually* (orientation) in and through free decisions whereby persons slowly determine the course of their lives. All the basic considerations treated in Part I are crucial for our approach here.

Sex, sexuality, and sexual behavior can be evaluated morally only by considering: 1) the fact that *persons* are involved, 2) the *relationship* that exists between persons, and 3) whether the meaning of the behavior harmonizes with the relationship, i.e., promotes its growth. This evaluation can be guided by a discussion of three principles, as follows.

First, sexuality cannot be considered separate from human persons. Human *persons* are sexual. Mary Jo is a woman; Bob is a man. They live, feel, think, speak, act as this woman, this man. Sex cannot be considered in isolation, divorced from the awareness (or ignorance), judgment (or irresponsibility), love (or hate) of human persons.

As unique persons we live in the concrete here and now, in Dayton, Ohio, U.S.A., in 1973. We do not exist simply as a nature, a body, or a spirit. We are persons, and this means many things.

Our "spiritness" enables us to be aware of ourselves and others (intelligence) and also to love and be loved (freedom). Each of us is a unique person, yet we discover our identity and grow as persons in relation with other persons, Mom and Dad, teacher and friend.

Our "bodyness" situates us in time and space; it enables us to communicate with other persons; it enables us to be emotional persons, to tremble with rage and be moved to pity. In short, everything about us, including our sexuality, is in terms of our being human persons.

Now, it is this unique *person* who is sexual. Every person is either a man or a woman — is sexual. Sex is not something I "have" and can turn on or off at will. I *can* and ought to control all the ways I express myself, e.g., anger, fear, aggression, and the ways that are more obviously sexual. But the point is, these are all expressions of *me*, a sexual person. At any moment, in all that we are and do, each of us acts as this *man,* this *woman,* i.e., as sexual persons.

Sexuality, then, should *not* be considered primarily or solely in terms of intercourse or marriage or procreation. These are not the *only* manifestations of sexuality. Mary Jo, Bob and many others may never engage in intercourse, may never get married, may never procreate. Yet they remain as fully sexual persons as those who do, and they can and will express themselves as men and women. The sexual dimension will be present and operative, though perhaps not so obviously as in intercourse.

To color every consideration of human sexuality in terms of marriage precludes a balanced appreciation not only of sexuality but of marriage itself. Sexuality is bigger and more basic than marriage. Every person is called to full maturity, including psychosexual, whether he or she enters marriage or not. Married partners engaging in intercourse must somehow be expressing their personal love for each other, or else they betray themselves as persons, and also marriage itself. Intercourse, genital arousal, is not only the expression of sexuality, but, much more importantly, the expression of love between married *persons*. Torn asunder from this relationship of love, intercourse itself is inhuman, immoral.

Our point is basic: sexuality, sexual expressions, sexual behavior must be seen in terms of *persons*.

Before we go on, it is important to point out another conclusion from this fact that we are sexual persons; namely, that *sexual* identity and maturing are inseparably bound up with *personal* identity and maturing. In a way, the sexual dimension is the most obvious criterion of personal identity and growth.

Since all growth takes time, we must allow time and opportunity for all persons, and obviously the young, to mature personally-sexually. One process

cannot happen without the other. The young especially will urgently need to grow in valuing their
sexuality precisely in terms of their development as
free, responsible, loving persons. Guidelines and
rules will be very helpful, but only if they are rooted
in a positive outlook and if they are broad enough
to allow for growth and development.

*Second, sexuality must be seen in terms of a loving
relationship.* Our two basic assumptions here are
that human persons are essentially *relational,* and
secondly, that the only morally good way that persons relate is in a *loving* way. Hence, human sexuality must be viewed in terms of a loving relationship between human persons, or lack of it.

Human persons can exist in many ways and do
many things that do not *immediately* involve other
persons. I can be alone on a mountain, or studying,
resting, painting, etc. But our assumption implies
that however we exist, whatever we do, we ever
remain persons oriented to other persons.

Even if I am alone on a mountain, unless I am
extremely selfish, it is impossible not to think of
other persons. In fact, perhaps the greatest benefit
of being alone on the mountain would be the clearer
view it affords me of the persons in my life. If I rest,
it is to be restored for continuing my life with other
people. If I paint a picture, I will want to show it to
someone, or at least communicate to someone the
fruit of my experience.

The application to our topic can be spelled out
this way: first, *sexuality* is an essential part of
being a human person; second, *relationship* is an

essential part of being a person. All human beings are sexual; all human beings need to be in relation to other persons.

This is not to say that we are always *aware* of the sexual dimension, or that it is always perceptibly manifest. Indeed, such is not the case in very many of our relationships. When Grandma relates to grandson, Dad relates to daughter, brother relates to sister, there is hardly any awareness of the sexual dimension. But it is there. When professional persons and clients relate, there is usually little or no awareness of the sexual dimension. But it is there. When persons of the same sex relate to each other, they are usually not aware to any appreciable degree of the sexual dimension. But it is there.

In fact, the deepest meaning of sexuality is that we need *other* people; we need other human beings to "complete" us. The sexual dimension is usually present to some significant degree, and at times very much so, when teenagers and adults relate to persons of the opposite sex. This is not only natural, it is important for human growth. Men and women are deeply complementary to each other. In a deep and usually somewhat heightened way, we grow in awareness of ourselves and our sexuality through relationships with persons of the other sex.

Our second assumption, discussed in Part I, is that for persons to be fully mature and psychologically and spiritually healthy, their relationships are to be *loving* ones — guided by faith in Christ and the circumstances of the present situation.

Again, therefore, to make the obvious explicit:

Since human persons are essentially sexual, and since they are healthy and growing as persons only when their relationship is at least basically loving, *sexual development is healthy and normal only in loving relationships.*

Some of our relationships may seem highly impersonal; for example, writing to Burpee's for a seed catalogue, or getting a uniform in a boot-camp lineup. But it is impossible to be completely neutral or indifferent toward anyone in the world — even those I have never met. I have a prior attitude that will assert itself, say next year, when I find myself at table with a Japanese businessman or a Jewish actress. I will either treat them respectfully or not. I cannot decide they do not exist, or that they have no claim on my attitude.

What does it mean, then, that as sexual persons we are all to relate to each other in a personally constructive, loving way?

Love is a very ambiguous term, and it has been used to cover a multitude of deceptions. We assume here that if it is to be genuine, authentic and real, it must have these characteristics at least in a basic way: 1) *Acceptance* of persons as valuable —as they are, and no matter who they are, seeing beneath the surface to the dignity God gives every person. 2) *Respect* for all the good — and all the potential for good — in every person: goodness, beauty, virtue, freedom, intelligence, sincerity, etc. 3) *Responsibility and care,* a willingness to put oneself at the disposal of the other for the good of the other. 4) *Fidelity and trust,* some steadfastness in affirming the goodness of the other, and some con-

tinuing confidence that this person can reach his or her potential. 5) *Gentleness,* some appreciation of the mystery of the other, and a warmth of affection coloring our acceptance, respect, care and trust. 6) *Communication,* some kind of personal sharing, giving and receiving.

Not all these aspects need be present in a vividly conscious way or in a fully developed form. But if a relationship is to be truly personal and loving, it must involve these qualities to some degree.

The conclusion is crucially important. Since human sexuality is totally pervasive of the human person, to be sexual is to be a loving person. Not to be a loving person is not only to fail as persons, but to fail as *men,* as *women.* To love is to be a true and normal *man,* a real and genuine *woman.*

Third, expressions of sexuality must be understood and evaluated in terms of the expression of love between persons. As human persons, we behave, act and express ourselves in endless ways. We laugh, cry, whisper, shout, shake hands, embrace, etc. Often we express ourselves in a loving way — a smile, a comforting word, listening, a helping hand, a gentle touch; sometimes in unloving ways — a harsh word, a rash judgment, betrayal of a confidence, breaking a promise, etc. But always we are expressing *ourselves.* All these expressions (what is done) must be seen and evaluated in terms of the persons involved, their relationship and what love demands. Striking a child may be an act of cruelty or an expression of parental love.

We are men-persons or women-persons; we are

related as men and women; we express ourselves as men or women; we love and hate as men or women. Some of the ways we express ourselves so involve the sexual dimension of our personal existence that we call those expressions "sexual." These are especially moments involving a heightened awareness of man-ness or woman-ness, or when I experience feelings, desires, touches, actions of a more obvious sexual nature.

Now, any attempt at moral evaluation of "sexual expressions" must face the fact that our very language is misleading. We speak as if sex is something we "have," something "added" to our personality, something that can be "used" more or less independently. From all we have tried to say about the meaning of person, it should be evident that there are no "merely" sexual expressions — as such. There are only expressions of personal love or hate of other persons that have (inevitably) a sexual aspect. Sometimes the latter is very obvious or intense, at other times it is scarcely noticeable.

Consequently it is never enough to know what persons are doing. We must know who the persons are and what their relationships are.

For example, all married couples have friends who are married. A married man may have a good or a bad reason for taking another man's wife to lunch. It may be the sign of a warm and healthy friendship that he kisses her as he arrives for the party; it *can* be a sign of an improper relationship between them. The point is, the external action can be judged morally only in terms of the total relationship and attitude of persons.

Again, an engaged couple express their deep and committed love in ways that are appropriate to them: they are not married, and they are not merely enjoying a first date. The moral risk they run is countered by their growing maturity and self-discipline. But what is appropriate for them may be irresponsible and dangerous for another couple who have no thought of marriage, or who are already seriously threatened by problems of maturing.

Again, there may be two people who are single and vowed to celibacy who have become very close friends over the years. They have no intention of ever marrying. They are a man and a woman, and they love each other deeply as a Christian man and woman. As human persons they express their love in many ways. But at no time do they act as though they were married, or express their love in a way that does not "fit" their relationship as two single persons vowed to celibacy.

In all three examples, a conscientious evaluation of expression of love is made according to the facts: who the persons are, their maturity or weakness and their commitments — to marriage, to celibacy, to future marriage, to work, etc. They seek to be open and realistic, aware of the goodness and meaning of their friendship, aware of what they are saying and what they are not saying in their expressions of love, and of what fits and does not fit their relationship.

For example, when a 17-year-old boy and girl express themselves on their third date in prolonged and passionate kissing and embracing, they are failing to reckon with the superficiality of their relationship or their own immaturity. Their behavior does not fit them. Or, when a married man and single woman engage in sexual intimacies, *what* they are doing and *what* they are saying may appear loving, but their expressions do not "fit" who they are or their commitments (he is married; she is not committed to him). Accordingly these expressions of themselves are immoral.

Now let's turn to some concrete questions in the area of sexuality and consider them briefly in the light of what we discussed in Part I and in this chapter.

Masturbation, sometimes called "self-abuse," involves full sexual arousal and orgasm apart from intercourse. Statistics, as well as the experience of confessors, indicate that masturbation is a *very* common difficulty. Until 10 or 15 years ago it was the almost unanimous opinion of theologians that masturbation was objectively (materially) a grave matter. Accordingly, if a person performed this action with full knowledge and full freedom, he was said to be guilty of mortal sin.

Because of this view, and because of the frequency of masturbation, it is easy to understand how deep was the feeling of guilt and hopelessness experienced by those who masturbated. They felt something was seriously wrong with them. Try as they might to avoid masturbation, some just never seemed to be successful. Accordingly, they tended to become hopelessly fearful and guilty and mistrustful of self, or to develop a "what's the use" attitude. In both instances they were "caught." At best they found themselves in and out of "mortal" sin rather frequently (if they still went to confession).

Of course, there was some awareness that the "full knowledge and full consent" necessary for mortal sin was often lacking. But the continual stress on the *objective* seriousness of masturbation in itself made it difficult or impossible for most people to judge that they were not seriously guilty. They were left with the impression that if they only tried harder they could avoid all problems in the matter. It was all very depressing.

In recent years masturbation has been seriously re-evaluated. Some serious deficiencies in past understanding and moral treatment of this difficulty have come to light. In addition, the primary focus today in any moral assessment of masturbation is on the *person.* The basic moral question concerns *who* this person is, the basic orientation of the person's life, the attitudes and habitual dispositions. In light of this, we can look at *what* the person is *doing* and make a moral judgment — first, about the goodness or badness of the actions and then about the guilt or non-guilt of the person.

In the case of masturbation great attention must be given to personal-sexual growth and development, or the lack of it. Masturbation by a 15-year-old boy is not the same as that masturbation of a 30-year-old married man. It is also necessary to reckon with the pressures and tensions which almost everyone, especially teenagers, experience in present day society. Finally, it is necessary to be aware that masturbation is often a *symptom* of personality problems, such as insecurity, guilt complex, hostility. If such is the case, it is fruitless to focus on the act of masturbation and leave the cause untouched.

This is not to treat masturbation casually, or to say it is good. But it is to say that masturbation is wrong (objectively) to the extent that it hinders personal, intersubjective, heterosexual growth. The focus is on the *person* and the person's basic responsibility to grow and develop, to be able to relate as fruitfully as possible to other persons as men and women.

Everyone is called to full Christian life. Everyone, therefore, is obliged to grow and develop as persons, as men and women able to relate to others in a way that is mature, fruitful, loving. Accordingly, because masturbation either directly or indirectly (e.g., when symptomatic of deeper personal problems) tends to hinder psychosexual development, it is morally unacceptable. Hence we are obliged to avoid it. Whether or not, and to what degree a person who engages in masturbation will be guilty of *sin* must be judged in the light of Chapter Four.

Another question much discussed today is premarital intercourse.

First of all, the term itself leaves much to be desired. It refers to the act of intercourse engaged in prior to marriage. Thus it embraces everything from selfish, unloving, inhuman intercourse with a prostitute to an act of intercourse between a man and woman who love each other and are engaged to enter marriage. Morally there is a vast difference in these situations when we consider the act of intercourse in terms of the persons involved and their relationship.

The second remark is this: the big argument of the past for the immorality of premarital intercourse was the danger of procreation outside of marriage. As there are many ways of preventing conception today, this argument holds little weight for most people.

It is my conviction, as well as that of most people, that past reasons for condemning premarital intercourse are seriously inadequate. Perhaps the greatest reason for this lies in our failure to appreciate positively the value and pervasive character of our human sexuality in terms of our personal and interpersonal existence. Only thus can we grasp the disorder, the negation of this value, in certain sexual expressions. This re-evaluation has begun. Theologians and psychologists are probing more deeply the *meaning* of sexual intercourse between human persons, particularly as expressive of interpersonal love, communication and fidelity.

One thing should be emphasized: our Catholic moral tradition has always involved the clear and definite teaching that every act of intercourse between unmarried persons is gravely disordered and at least objectively immoral. This is a fact. It may not mean much to some, particularly to those for whom membership in the Church, the believing community, is unimportant. But this is a fact we must reckon with. The Church is saying that the *only* personal relationship that the act of intercourse is able to *express* is the relationship of love between a man and woman permanently, exclusively and totally given to each other in marriage. Only such a relationship can symbolize the union between Christ and his Church. Only such a relationship *demands* the total love, fidelity and life-giving character which intercourse, by its nature, signifies. Thus intercourse, as an expression of love, "fits" only those who are married to each other.

As we have said (perhaps ad nauseam) sexual expressions come out of the relationship between persons. Premarital intercourse is unacceptable because it cannot express a lifelong commitment before God to a loving, exclusive, stable relationship, or express a willingness to accept all the responsibilities and consequences of such a relationship. All this is simply stated in the wedding vows, "for richer, for poorer; in sickness and in health; until death do us part." Such a commitment is a marriage commitment. When such a decision has *not* been made — and, by Christians, sealed sacramentally — the lives of the couple are entirely premarital. They do not have a reason or right to act as married persons.

We said above that a loving relationship between two persons has the qualities of acceptance, respect, responsibility, care, faithfulness, trust, gentleness and personal sharing. All of these can be present in both marital and premarital relationships of love. But one factor makes the one essentially different from the other: *permanence,* freely chosen, especially in a sacramental context. Man and wife accept and respect each other as permanent life partners in Christ — "until death do us part." Such a lifelong commitment *is* a marriage commitment and this particular expression of sexual love does not fit persons who have not made this commitment. Hence premarital sex is disordered, contrary to a responsible moral attitude. It cannot in this case be the expression of mature Christian love.

Note that we are not implying that every act of intercourse between unmarried persons involves mortal guilt, especially for the engaged. We have stated that sexual intercourse between unmarried persons is a gravely disordered *act*. But whether or not, and to what degree, these particular persons who engage in extramarital intercourse are guilty of sin must be evaluated in the light of Chapter Four.

Note also that we are not saying that a "piece of legal paper" (marriage license) makes sexual intercourse okay. Married persons can engage in intercourse in ways that are unloving, impersonal and inhuman. But we are saying that intercourse between married persons can "fit" their conjugal relationship and express the unique love and fidelity of such a relationship, and thus be good, true and beautiful.

Finally, granting the position of the Catholic Church that premarital intercourse is (objectively) gravely disordered, and granting that there is a presumption that those who engage in premarital intercourse incur guilt, the following questions are still crucial to any full moral evaluation of personal guilt: *who* are these persons, *what* is their *relationship;* what are they seeking to communicate and *why;* and how does their sexual expression harmonize with all this? As with all moral judgments, we must view all actions in the light of the basic life-orientation, moral awareness and freedom of persons. Only when we take all these things into consideration can a judgment be made as to the presence and the degree of moral goodness or guilt.

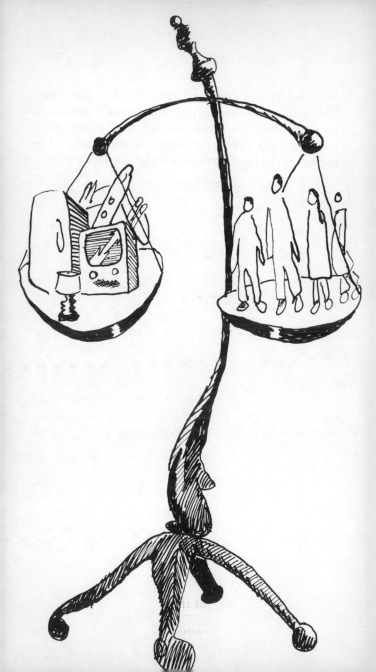

Chapter X

JUSTICE

We now turn to a consideration of justice, the value underlying the Seventh and Tenth Commandments.

In the first section of this book we saw that the new approach to morality has as its primary focus the human person in relationship, building community and social solidarity. Such an approach has profound consequences for our understanding of justice.

We also considered freedom and responsibility as characteristically stressed in the new approach to morality; in particular, that dimension of responsibility which altogether precludes an individualistic approach and emphasizes the *social* aspect. This too has far-reaching consequences for our understanding and practice of justice. Let us explore this briefly.

Our understanding of justice has been excessively narrow and individualistic; it has been too centered on *things,* too much divorced from love. The *social* dimension of justice has been recognized, but the main concern, especially in the past century, has been *commutative* justice, the rendering in strict measure what one individual owes to another, e.g., paying just debts, returning borrowed property, fulfilling contracts. This is well and good. But there are more basic aspects of justice which look to *persons, social* ramifications and *institutional* dimensions.

As Christians we have no choice but to consider these larger aspects. The narrower view of commutative justice alone may actually *result in injustice.* For example, an apartment owner may seem, in a narrow sense, to have a right to payment of rent and the renter an obligation in justice to pay rent. But if the apartments are unfit for human habitation, the owner may be unjust in demanding any payment of rent. What is more, he may well be extremely unjust in not respecting the dignity and rights of the poor persons who live in his apartment. The apartment owner may be guilty of inhuman and immoral extortion, even though in a narrow and superficial sense he has a right in justice to payment for use of his property. Before God, if not before the civil law, he may be guilty of many wrongs that far outweigh his "rights."

This example illustrates how our understanding of justice has been too "thing-centered," too concerned with *what* is owed and with the individual right to own and control property. "Pay what you owe" can be indicative of great injustice precisely because it focuses on material things and ignores persons. When "justice" is understood too much in terms of material goods, it can become distorted and vicious. When the right to amass and dispose of private property is held to be practically absolute, terribly inhuman and immoral consequences result: some men can become multimillionaires while countless other men lack the necessities of life. Unless the wealth of this world is seen as given by God *for all men,* the abuse of private ownership will continue to breed injustice. The popes have stressed this more and more forcibly. In the last half-century their warnings culminated in the documents of Vatican II, Pope Paul's encyclical *Populorum Progressio,* and the justice document of the 1971 Roman Synod. But so far this crucially important social teaching of our Church seems to play second-fiddle to discussion of the pill.

Justice has been distorted because it has been separated from love. Somehow, strangely, the impression has prevailed among many Catholics that one can be *just yet unloving,* or that one can be *loving but unjust,* as if the two values lived in separate airtight compartments.

But justice is always and necessarily interrelated with love. Love is absolute and irreplacable. All other values and virtues must somehow be expressions of it. If justice is to be a Christian value, it must be a justice of love or it is not justice at all. To pay a debt of money in a way that is disrespectful to the lender and to consider the payment an "act of justice" while violating the lender's most basic right to respect as a person, is to make nonsense of the meaning of justice.

It is important to be concerned about paying debts and fulfilling contractual requirements, etc. But there is urgent need to be more concerned about justice on a more basic level — particularly in terms of poor, deprived, unemployed, uneducated, handicapped *people*. It is not only a matter between individuals. The greatest injustice is perpetrated by institutions, the complex systems men devise to seek their purposes. Injustice can be built into the very culture and social customs of a nation. The injustice thus caused to persons is all the more serious because of the seeming "righteousness" of those who inflict or tolerate it, the apparent legality that surrounds it, and the great difficulty of changing the status quo.

Discriminatory housing patterns are supported by people who "want only what is best for their children" and who desire to "maintain quality education"; deceit in government is approved by all who "realize" that you have to cut a few corners to get some place in this world; trade arrangements that keep developing countries in a state of poverty are made in the name of keeping our economy healthy, maintaining a balance of payments.

To repeat, these injustices may seem relatively unimportant because our focus has been on property, possessions and material goods. We practically equate injustice with theft, robbery, arson, vandalism, etc. Almost nothing is considered worse in America today than the destruction of our sacred property. Nothing can justify doing *that,* though we are not too hard pressed to find justification for the destruction of persons by built-in denial of their rights to education and employment, by inhumane treatment, by double standards for men and women, blacks and whites — not to speak of finding it unavoidable to bomb civilians (foreigners) and abort babies (ours).

The greatest injustice is done to persons, not things, by denying them what everyone has a *right* to: respect, dignity and equal opportunity in the basic areas of food, housing, education, jobs, status as citizens. Unless we pursue justice for all, we betray the virtue we profess to believe in. "Law and order" can be twisted into a program for continuing injustice.

But people say, "I work for what I get! I pay my debts, and I don't steal from anybody." The implication is that I have done all that is required by the Seventh and Tenth Commandments: "I am not doing anybody any injustice." But a Christian also works so that others may "get"; he gladly pays his debt of concern for the personal welfare of others, especially those in physical, emotional, intellectual or moral need. His "not-stealing" covers both his neighbor's wallet and personal dignity.

If we can break out of our narrow concept of injustice, we may discover that it is the broad and silent injustices that finally cause anger, frustration and despair to explode in violence, robbing, burning and killing. One kind of violence leads to another.

To attempt mere external control of one type of violence and not the other is a waste of time. To attempt merely to put down external violence by force is to treat symptoms instead of causes. It is like using a strait-jacket to cure convulsions.

In other areas — the drug problem, prostitution, graft — it is again the underlying causes that need our attention, for it is there that the basic "injustice" may be found.

Even the sanctuary of "law" and "order," our legal and court system, has contributed to widespread if disguised injustice. In the land that is supposedly devoted to justice and freedom for all, it is simply not true that a poor man gets the same legal protection as a rich man. It is a fact of life that a poor black man or a drifter is often not "presumed innocent until proven guilty."

As we come to see the true nature of justice, we might also recognize our part in fostering such injustices, particularly by silent acquiescence and failure to speak out. Perhaps we will come to the point of being willing to fight such deep injustices.

Justice demands that we re-evaluate those aspects of the capitalistic system which represent an unbridled quest for profit and the use of persons as mere instruments of the process. Can we take for granted that "business is business," that ruthless individualism is the name of the game and that it's just too bad that some people get hurt in a competitive society?

Many things that go on in the name of "modern business" fly in the face of the principle emphasized by popes for the last hundred years: namely, the goods and resources of the earth are given by God *primarily* to *all* men. Only if this principle is being followed does anyone have the right to own or control material wealth.

Another way a distorted notion of justice finds expression is: "I worked hard for what I got, and it's mine; let all those lazy people work and get theirs; if they don't work, it's their own fault." There is truth here, but it is so oversimplified that it betrays the justice it supposedly expresses. We assume that people who want to work can find work. We assume that people who want decent housing can find it, and at a reasonable price. We assume that educational opportunities are equally available and equally good. We assume that anyone who really wants to can lift himself and his family by the boot straps from long-suffered social misery, exclusion, deprivation; from family life destroyed by poverty, despair and the prison of the ghetto.

We listen with sympathy to the complaints of middle-class people about high taxes, the high cost of living, high food prices, exorbitant cost of labor and services, the injustice of manufacturers' "built-in obsolescence." But do we really appreciate how much *more* reason for complaint the poor have? Starting with much less, they also must pay the same high prices for food, clothing, housing, medicine, etc. Do we have any sense of their intolerable frustration, the numbing sense of powerlessness they must experience as they face this situation year after year, with no real hope that it will ever get better? No wonder some people become cynical, bitter, mean or violent.

Of course, if we merely look at the objective fact of violence, we immediately say, "That's bad!" But it would be a terrible oversimplification to say these *people* are violent and bad. They may feel that only through violence can they get a hearing. When violence is the last desperate effort of anyone whose personal dignity has been ground down almost to nothing, it assumes a very different moral quality and may be seen by them as morally good.

It is critically necessary for us to examine our culture and its lopsided glorification of power, wealth, and status which fosters so much cutting of corners, gouging, fleecing, bribing — so much abuse of people! It is urgent for us to reassess our cultural approval and high regard for "success," materially measured, and contempt for "failure," also materially measured. We need to examine our indifference, complacency and smugness about the *fact* that millions in our own country not only lack the basic necessities of life, but have no real opportunity to get them. Someday each of us must render an account of how we have used our energy, talents, time and *possessions* in feeding the hungry, giving drink to the thirsty, clothing the naked, sheltering the homeless and freeing the imprisoned. Christ's condemnation at the last judgment (Matthew 25) is to fall on those who did *not* do something for the hungry and naked, the prisoners and the strangers.

It is time for Catholics to move! Time to *listen* to what the Church has been telling us, especially in the last decade. It is time to put the pill and contraception and other less important matters in their place and really become concerned, courageously and effectively, about social justice, the basic dignity and rights of every human person. There is little time left.

This clear call to action for justice was repeated by the Pope and the bishops at the 1971 Synod in Rome. "Action on behalf of justice and participation in the transformation of the world fully appear to us as a *constitutive dimension of the preaching of the Gospel*. . . . Witnessing to justice demands a total renewal of the life-style and practice of the Church, both in the organizational life of its institutions and in the daily life of its members."

The Synod emphatically reminds us that "action for justice" is a *constitutive* dimension of the preaching of the Gospel. In plain words, if Catholics do not talk and act for social justice, something essential is missing from their religion. Action for justice is not just a "nice" thing, a luxury for those who like that sort of thing. Still less is it "politics," which "has no place" in morality and religion. It is necessary to our endeavor to live the Gospel.

The Synod is quick to point out that action for justice demands a deep change in our hearts and in our lives: total renewal. This includes reform of organizational life of some institutions within the Church so that there will be equal consideration for all, reasonable speed in the hearing of marriage cases, the payment of just wages to all, decent working conditions and participation in the decisions that affect workers' lives. It is not just in the secular world that injustice is destroying people. Catholics and Catholic institutions have practiced and fostered injustice too. *Our* life-style, our behavior, must be totally renewed.

It's noteworthy that the bishops call for "*action*

for justice." We have had enough words. It is time to *do* something. It is the same urgent demand for action that St. John stresses: "Let us not love in word alone, but in deed." It is the same demand St. James makes when stressing that faith without works is dead, or when he calls that religion "vain and useless" which does not aid and defend widows and orphans, i.e., the helpless ones. As the Synod put it, ". . . anyone who ventures to speak to people about justice must first *be* just." We must put our money and our life where our mouth is. We must not betray the Gospel by following the life-style of a world where injustice abounds. "Hence," the bishops continue, "we must undertake an examination of the modes of acting, of the possessions, and the life-style found within the Church herself. . . ." Anything less only destroys our credibility.

"Christian love of neighbor and justice cannot be separated," the Synod continues. "Love makes an absolute demand for justice in the recognition of the dignity and rights of one's neighbor. Justice attains its inner fullness only in love. . . . For unless the Christian message of love and justice shows its effectiveness through action in the cause of justice in the world, it will only with difficulty gain credibility with the men of our times."

Such words need no comment. It seems evident that it is not book or classroom or lecture education that we need. Rather, we need to be sensitized to concrete injustice and thus educated in a way that arouses us to act. This means an education that involves actually experiencing in some way the situations in which injustice exists, entering into the lives of the people who are suffering. If such experiences do not make clear the way we should go, nothing else will.

The *Center of Concern,* based in Washington, D.C., has launched an ecumenical effort primarily for Americans to organize and act on behalf of the poor and powerless of the world. One of the very noteworthy hopes of the Center is that the quest for justice becomes the common cause of all American Catholics.

The earthquake change in the world — and therefore in the Church — has shaken and confused many Catholics. Misinformation and fear have so polarized American Catholics that at least some of them have doubts about their identity as a Church. Perhaps by joining in concern for others they can find unity among themselves.

Action for justice can take many forms. Here we indicate a few that seem basic. It means, first, that we practice justice in our own lives. We need to examine, and very likely *change,* our life-style. The Gospel calls us to poverty of spirit, simplicity of life, freedom from domination by material goods. We need to be sparing, precisely in order to share with others. At first glance, most Catholics seem quite surprised at such a suggestion. "We have to struggle *now* to make ends meet and pay our bills. How can you suggest that we live more sparingly?"

Yet a closer look at our life-style reveals that most of us could live much more simply.

We have to examine our "needs" very rigorously. These "needs" are so often dictated, in fact contrived, by the assumed demands of social status, middle class "values," and the massive hypnosis of advertising.

Our "needs" have been grossly exaggerated. One sharp practitioner in the world of selling recently said, "The principle we operate on is that the people are always 'wrong' — that is, they really don't need this thing they're buying, but by the time they begin to catch on, we'll have something new that they don't need!"

Page through a magazine or your daily newspaper and decide how many things, or at least how many things *that* expensive, you need for a decent, cultured, Christian life that declares itself to be modeled on the Gospel. (*Nobody* needs a $19 electric denture cleaner!) Consider the need, or the need for this quality, of household furnishings, toiletries, liquor, clothing, "extras" in automobiles, labor saving devices, gadgets, adult or children's playthings. We could do with much less without in the least jeopardizing our health or being reduced to anywhere near real want.

A more sparing life would free us from our growing dependence on material things and free us for a *greater awareness* and concern for persons.

Also, when we look at the actual situation in the Church and its institutions in the U.S., there are appalling evidences of wastefulness. Such wastefulness takes on the evil of injustice when seen in terms of the poverty and want of so many. In our dioceses, in our parishes, in religious communities, in our schools, in our hospitals, etc., there is an excessive amount of duplication and waste involving not only buildings and equipment, but also personnel, efforts, energy, time, talent and money.

For example, we find two neighboring parishes failing, even refusing, to cooperate in planning and administering schools, CCD programs, adult education programs. We find Catholic seminaries still operating independently and endeavoring to carry on a full educational program for fewer than 100 students. Similar situations exist with regard to Catholic colleges, hospitals, etc. Many expensive buildings stand empty; large tracts of property lie idle. It seems intolerable that the waste in buildings, land, money, equipment and personnel should continue. Such a massive situation of injustice and unacceptable stewardship is in urgent need of attention when so many people all around us lack even the bare necessities for a decent, human life.

The question of the life-style of bishops, priests and religious calls for change in attitude and practice. These members of the Church above all are to reflect in their lives the values of the Gospel, poverty of spirit and detachment as a means to generous sharing. Yet what usually is apparent is a life-style that is very comfortably "middle-class" in residence, dress, car, meals, recreation — sometimes combined with a lack of active concern for the poor, the helpless, the deprived.

The Church must face the question of ensuring just wages in its institutions, respect for the rights of women, real participation of the laity in decision making, freedom of speech, due process for the accused. There are many issues involving the dignity

149

and the rights of persons in the Church and they call for action.

In summary, let us repeat: justice cannot be rightly understood apart from persons. Justice in the deepest sense means recognizing and respecting the dignity of every human person. Only if we respect the dignity of a person can we give him what is his due. Justice cannot be separated from love, for it is the embodiment of effective, human and Christ-like love for all persons.

Justice, then, can never be equated with paying bills or fulfilling contracts, and certainly not with the control and amassing of wealth or power. Justice can never be limited only to what goes on between individuals. It must also characterize the existence and operation of human institutions and organizations.

The value and virtue underlying the Seventh and Tenth Commandments is justice. This value presupposes that love is the primary moral absolute and that we show our love for God by loving our neighbor, without exception, as Jesus loves us. Accordingly, justice mediates love. It presupposes that all the goods and wealth of the world are from God for all men. It cries out against all the ways in which persons are deprived, degraded, dehumanized, disrespected, mistreated, looked down upon, taken advantage of; against the fact that so many people do not have sufficient housing, jobs, food, clothing, medical care or education to lead a life befitting them as human persons.

There is urgent need to become more sensitive to widespread injustices and to see that they stem not only from individual failure, but perhaps even more from institutional and organizational weakness in both Church and state. There is urgent need, most of all by all of us who profess to be Catholics, to take note of these injustices, to take a stand and to take action.

Chapter XI

LIVING IN THE TRUTH

When our moral focus shifts from nature to person, the very concept of truth undergoes an important change. In the past, "truth" was excessively objectified, "out there" somewhere. Once we discovered it "out there," we captured it in sentences, and then we "had" the truth. Indeed, we defined truth as the correspondence between what is in the mind and what is outside the mind (objective reality). This approach is reflected in our understanding of faith as an assent of the *mind* to formulated propositions about God, and in our excessive stress on the unchangeableness of truth once captured in propositions.

Such a view obscures the fact that truth is experienced only by living persons. It is a quality of the awareness and appreciation of reality by this or that given person who seeks or embraces truth, and whose whole personal makeup affects their experience. An excessively objectified understanding of truth does not pay sufficient attention to the fact that our personal search for truth is always historically conditioned by the cultural and social conditions in which we exist. A first-century Christian approached the search for truth from an experience much different from that of a 20th-century Catholic. Moreover, truth is experienced quite differently by a person dying of cancer, a philosopher in his study, a senator running for office, and a mother of teenagers.

A static notion of truth sees it as granite — the unchangeable, unshakable foundation of life. There is no doubt that this approach has merit and has served many people well. But it is not the whole story. Truth is the reflection of the infinite God, whose height and depth and breadth of life will always beckon man to deeper insights, like an ever-widening horizon. Man grows in appreciation and the joy of never-ending discovery.

Accordingly, as our focus shifts to the person, we become clearly aware that no one sentence or book, no one mere human being, can ever "possess" the fullness of truth on any given matter at any given time. We grasp truth in a personal, historical, developing way.

Now, lest this seem to imply that we must live on shaky probabilities, let it be stressed that we do have convictions, and that these can be expressed in sentences. We do grasp truth, most importantly in faith. But we need not overestimate our grasp of truth and our ability to express it. Neither should we underestimate our obligation to an ongoing effort to grow in truth.

All this has concrete implications when we consider the violation of truth: lying. In the traditional moral approach, our faculty of speech was considered in terms of this objectified understanding of truth. A lie occurred when speech ("out there") expressed something contrary to what was in the mind. A lie was considered morally evil because it violated the function of speech thus understood.

The newer approach to morality sees speech in terms of persons communicating with each other. Lying, in this view, is evil because it is deceitful and destructive of the trust and confidence necessary for human community. The seriousness of lying is measured by the degree of its destructiveness to trust between persons. It is primarily the relationship between persons that is morally decisive, not the *mere* fact that my words do or do not objectively convey what is in my mind.

A significant change in the teaching of the Church will serve as an example of what happens when we shift the emphasis from nature to person. Some 20 years ago Pius XII taught that religious and moral error had no right to exist or be propagated. From an abstract and objective viewpoint, such teaching is understandable. What right has "2 + 2 = 5" or "Communism must prevail" to exist "out there"? We Catholics acted out such teaching, for example, in our very negative and often quite intolerant approach to non-Catholics.

However, John XXIII took a personal, pastoral point of view and taught just as strongly that human *persons* have a basic right and obligation to follow their consciences in religious and moral mat-

155

ters, and that this right must be respected, even if authorities or fellow citizens are certain that a person is *factually* wrong, as if he were to say that black is white. This position rests on the dignity, responsibility and freedom God gives every person.

Finally, it is also significant and reflective of what is happening in morality that young people are intensely concerned with truth in a personal sense (personal integrity, personal authenticity) more than their elders were. The young tend to become quite upset, "turned off" and disillusioned by any apparent smugness or complacency that says "we Catholics have the truth" and that others — benighted people — deserve only our pity, if not our disapproval. It seems contradictory to the young that so much stress should be placed on correct *words* and far less on *living* the truth, being authentic as persons, concerned with expressing in action the faith we profess with our lips. An excessively objectified understanding of the truth does tend to lead to hypocrisy, a chasm between what we say and what we do! The fact that the contradiction is "out there," i.e., not meant, only shows the depth of the problem.

So, let us reflect somewhat on the Eighth Commandment: "Thou shalt not bear false witness against thy neighbor." It is a negative statement to be understood in terms of the positive value of truthfulness.

Living in the Truth

Truthfulness in communication presupposes persons who love each other and want to be good for

156

each other, who accept reality, i.e., the call of God to respond freely to the needs of other persons.

Only with this in mind can we see the value — should we say the inevitableness? — of *speaking* the truth.

Jesus is the "Word" uttered eternally by the Father, truthfully reflecting in himself all that the Father is. He is the "Word" made flesh — a communicating to us by the Father.

What does it mean to say that Jesus is the truth? He is truth since he reveals who the Father is, and the life and love of the Father to us. He is truth since he embodies and reveals in himself all that we are called to become. He is our truth; he is the Father's truth.

The Father utters his Word in full personal love, the Holy Spirit; so also, the Son reflects perfectly all that the Father is in the Holy Spirit. So in Trinitarian life the truth is communicated in the fullness of personal love.

In God there is truth, love, fullness. In him they are inseparable; they are personal. Our life is a sharing of God's life: hence, "truth" is never something impersonal or abstract. It is a quality in the personal relationships of people who want to share the fullness of love as it is in God. Since God gives *his* life, not just "some kind of" life, a similar relationship of person, truth and love will also characterize the words and actions of Christians. If we are like God, we do not separate "truth" into a compartment sealed off from other compartments marked "love" and "persons."

157

Being in the Truth

The value underlying and demanded by the Eighth Commandment, therefore, is to be seen in light of Jesus who is our truth, and in whom we are personally called to live in the truth.

To the extent that we *are* in Christ, we are in the truth. To the extent we are not in Christ, to that extent we are still in sin and not yet the person we are called to become.

But, to *be* in the truth is dynamic, a matter of life, power and growth: we must be *living* expressions of Christ. We must seek to reflect in our lives the truth — the reality — who is Christ; inevitably this reflects Christ to the world. Since we are never *fully* alive in Christ, we must seek to grow, to become more fully who we are called to be. Truth requires growth.

"Not bearing false witness" means we must not cloud or distort, disguise or destroy the truth of our being by personal sin. Every personal sin is a lie, a failure to communicate who we really are, or are called to become, in Christ. In this sense, bad example is not only an unloving and harmful influence on others, it is a betrayal of *ourselves*, our personal truth. It is personal infidelity and moral phoniness. It is a betrayal of Christ, *our* truth.

Truth in Action

By our baptismal consecration our very being is caught up in Jesus. We must therefore *express* ourselves and *act* in a way that harmonizes with our "being in Christ." We must not betray in action what the truth of our being demands.

Thus, our life in Christ demands that we love others as Jesus loves us. So if at any time we fail to love others in this way, we are also untruthful in action. We are being untrue to our calling; we are not being true Christians. Likewise when we are unjust, impure, disobedient, or fail in any other way to act in harmony with our life in Christ, we are betraying in act the truth we are called to live. We are being inauthentic, phony. We are in a real sense "bearing false witness against our neighbor" because we are not giving him the *evidence* of Christ's presence within us. We are concealing reality — the way things really are between God and man; we are substituting a counterfeit way of acting. We deprive others of what they have a right to see: a *true* way of living.

In this perspective we may see a deeper meaning in the words of Paul, "See to it that you put an end to lying; let everyone speak the truth to his neighbor, for we are members of one another" (Eph. 4:25). The Eighth Commandment, particularly as seen in the light of Christ who is our Truth, demands far-reaching truthfulness of us. It has to do with much more than speech; it embraces all behavior, whereby we express (or fail to express) our personal life in Christ.

Truthfulness in Speech

If *all* the expressions of our life must be "truthful" (i.e., stem from and manifest our life in Christ), then we can appreciate the value of truthfulness in speech. We can grasp the evil of lying and all the unloving and unjust forms it can take:

deceit, detraction, slander, calumny.

Speech is one of the most common ways in which persons communicate. It can, of course, be very "uncommunicative," impersonal, merely informational; but at best it is one of the important and ordinary ways in which persons share and communicate themselves, go out in love to others, build community. It is one of the ordinary ways we come to know and love ourselves and others. Speech, then, is one of the important and necessary ways of fulfilling the foremost norm of morality — growing up and promoting the basic value of person and community. But speech will achieve this between persons only insofar as it involves us in a *loving communication* of the truth, a truthful communication of love. It is only by growing in love that we fulfill the Gospel. We dare not think ourselves unworthy or incapable of the actual life God has given us — his own. As the self-communication between Father and Son is always in the fullness of love — the Spirit — so must our human communication be.

When speech is untruthful, i.e., unloving, our dignity is betrayed. We fail to reflect God's goodness and truthfulness in what we are and what we do. We are inauthentic, insincere, phony, hypocritical, sinful.

In summary, "To maintain an adequate moral norm of 'true speech' we must go beyond the mere psychological concept of true speech (conformity of word to mind) and keep in mind the divine primordial pattern and the human end and purpose of the word. *The goal is the building up of love in our-*

selves, in our neighbor, in the community. Speech (in this term we include all signs and actions insofar as they 'express' something for our neighbor) must be community-forming and community-sustaining" (Bernard Häring, *Law of Christ,* III, 559).

Accentuating the Positive

As with all aspects of the new approach to morality, the emphasis should be on the positive: to communicate our truth lovingly. We should certainly *not* lie and thus sow the seeds of suspicion and mistrust among others. All the more we should *not* blacken the good name of others, bringing injustice on them. We should *not* talk about others in a way that reveals their hidden weaknesses and possible sinfulness or violates their trust and confidence.

But we are challenged by the virtue of truthfulness (Eighth Commandment) to do much more than avoid violations. We are challenged to commit ourselves to the *value* of truthfulness.

There are endless opportunities. Husbands and wives, for example, can nurture or heal their relationship by words consciously intended simply to please: a compliment, a sharing of feeling, a direct or indirect statement of forgiveness or apology. The patterns of sound that children learn from their parents gradually become patterns of life: words that express the joy of faith, the courage of faithfulness, the trust mixed with pain that make up the greater portion of most of our lives.

Words of good humor are the great lubricant of life. At work or at play, in offices or factories, in the car pool, before or during (especially during!) the PTA meeting or the what-are-they-teaching-our-kids confrontation, it is those who are able to find humor in the situation who are the peacemakers. Their words are *truth*.

Yet the warning and accusing prophets speak truth too, and we must respect them — at times join them — though their words touch us "where we live," in reality.

Sympathetic words to the suffering, encouraging words to the young, soft words to the angry, angry words to the soft — these are all ways in which we communicate truth to each other in charity.

Still broader areas of truth call for our attention. In the use of authority — federal, state and local — there is always great danger that men will distort the truth, *express* half-truths or downright lies under the guise of "protecting the best interest" of the people. Political "wisdom" is mere hypocrisy when it sacrifices truth to getting votes or maintaining power. There are surely times when the interest and safety of the people require secrecy. But the people have a basic right to know, and it is a serious violation of truthfulness in our civic life when the truth is not forthcoming, or worse, when it is deliberately distorted so as to mislead. The same kind of situation can be operative between the hierarchy and other members of the Church, between management and labor, between administration and students, parents and children.

Another area in which truthfulness is easily violated is advertising. The goal is — what else? — to get your money and make a profit. The merits and effectiveness of the product are sometimes so exaggerated as to border on the miraculous. False needs are created. I simply must have new clothes, more clothes, electric toothbrushes and sit-down lawnmowers. I may even be out of it if I don't have the latest translation of the Bible!

There is almost no end to the problems of truth. One of our country's basic building blocks is freedom of speech. It can be abused by those who reject any restraint of charity or justice. It can be abused by those with the power to buy off, scare off, or kill off those whose printed or spoken words would disclose injustice.

The right to privacy, i.e., to the enjoyment or preservation of personal truth and reality to which others have no right, is increasingly jeopardized in a technological society where wire-tapping, secret tape-recording, and telescopic photography have become commonplace.

Finally, each of us must examine our own speech. Not just for outright lying or slander, but to consider how much responsibility we show for what we pour into the ears of others. The unconsidered opinions we express at a moment's notice, the rumors we pass on; the jokes we tell, the countless words that are spoken with little or no regard for any real *purpose*.

If finally we have come to realize that it is possible to run out of clean air and water and to pollute our whole earth by sheer wasting of material resources, perhaps we will also come to realize that life can be polluted by a thoughtless waste of words: an almost automatic flow of sounds whereby we respond superficially and carelessly to persons around us. The fact that we are so used to it does not change the reality: careless speech is an indication that we don't place much value on the communication or the relationship — and therefore the person we are addressing.

Far from being a simple black-and-white matter, then, the Eighth Commandment for a Christian is another facet of a fundamental commitment to Christ: the desire to let all life — especially the unique gift of speech — be a careful and joyful expression of reality seen in the light of faith.

In time of war, truth is the first casualty. In the war on goodness, truth was the first casualty. The tempter said to Eve, "You will *not* die."

This was the Enemy — the literal meaning of "Devil" — the one Christ said was a "liar from the beginning." But the Word of the true God said, "I have come that you may have the truth, and the truth will make you free."

Epilogue

many feel that the "new" morality is an *easy* morality, catering to human weakness, leading to excessive permissiveness, and ultimately to immorality and licentiousness. This is unfounded and untrue. In fact, it seems to me that anyone who says or creates the impression that the "new" morality is an easier morality simply does not understand it. Perhaps it will be helpful to explore that idea.

Traditional morality, particularly as presented in the last 300 years, focused predominantly on conformity with human *nature* considered generally. From this understanding, general laws were deduced which told us precisely what we were obliged to do and not do if we were to avoid sin, especially mortal sin. From these general laws, many more particular ones were spelled out in detail. A quick look at any moral theology textbook published from 1650 to 1950 would basically confirm this. Examples are hardly needed. We need only recall our own moral instruction in school (grade, high, college), from the pulpit, in the confessional, in books and magazines. All this was most noticeable with regard to the obligation of Sunday Mass, fast and abstinence, servile work, and with regard to stealing, lying, impurity.

As a result, a very deep impression was made on most Catholics that the heart of Christian living consisted in obeying laws, and, therefore, avoiding sin. Even so, no one seemed very surprised that apparently there were still a lot of mortal sins committed. There was the confessional, thank God, and all we had to do was confess our mortal sins and promise to try again, and go away feeling very good (or very hopeless). We could even smile at the description of the "good" Catholic as one who went to Mass on Sunday, ate no meat on Friday, and put his envelope in the collection regularly. Charity simply meant selective almsgiving. You learned to "play it safe." Don't stick your neck out, don't rock the boat, do what you are told. Watch out for occasions of sin, avoid temptation. Don't scandalize anyone. Say your prayers, don't curse, pay your taxes, and all will be well.

This is a caricature of traditional morality, but it rings a lot of bells. There was much that was sound and good — as far as it went — especially when complemented by ascetical and mystical theology. But, somehow traditional morality was too impersonal, law-centered and preoccupied with sin. It tended to lull Catholics into a false sense of certainty and security. It was far too concerned with individual actions, especially the bad ones. It

167

was too little concerned with the overall dimensions of morality, with *doing* good. This is perhaps quite understandable in the light of the times, conditions of society, level of Christian education. But the fact is that for three centuries traditional morality did not reflect well the challenging demands of the Gospel. *The truth is that "traditional" morality was too easy,* gave a false sense of security, and in large measure led to attitudes that are un-Christian.

Our conviction is that the "new" morality is *not* easy, but very demanding. Norms, laws are necessary and helpful guides, but they cannot substitute for our personal responsibility. *We* will have to answer to God: no law will answer for us.

Focusing on person, the new morality is quite aware of human weakness and human sinfulness. The new morality is more concerned about avoiding *all* sin than was traditional morality. Hence, it stresses as *basic* to Christian life a wholehearted endeavor to convert, to be engaged in on-going conversion and repentance. The new morality sees sin as primarily not impurity, but as omission, as failure to love, to grow, to get involved, to *do* something about poverty, injustice, oppression, war; failure to be merciful, to love other persons as Jesus loves us. Accordingly the new morality stresses in every way that the most effective and fruitful way to repent, to be converted, to avoid and overcome sin, is *by doing good.* This is perfectly consistent with the Gospel, and precisely because it is positive and open-minded and undetermined, it demands tremendously *more* of the Catholic than does traditional morality. There are no simple, clear, definite rules. There is no end to the demands of love. When you have forgiven that 490th person, the 491st is waiting around the corner. When you have broken bread with 5000 people, the first of a new 5000 is getting ready to ring your doorbell.

In this sense there is nothing new about the new morality. It simply takes the Gospel literally and seriously: Love God and your neighbor and yourself with your *whole* heart, all the time. This is a very demanding kind of morality, precisely because God doesn't do things half-heartedly. He cannot say, "I don't really care if you're not like me, or if you waste half my gift in unhappiness." The God who literally gave his Son for us cannot expect anything less from us who have his life. Jesus really had no choice, being *true* God and man, but to say that we are to give our lives for our brothers and sisters, exactly as he did.

With focus on person, on love, on freedom and responsibility, the new morality requires much more of us in terms of faith and hope. It removes the false security of justification by good works, i.e., by keeping the Commandments. It removes the certainty that we know all the laws and precisely how to obey them, all the questions and all the answers. It stresses that our life rests on personal commitment to Jesus, personal allegiance to the Living God who demands that we come to *Him* in the darkness and uncertainty of faith. The new morality stresses the fact that we cannot place our hope in "horses and chariots," in observance of law and ritual, in human institutions. Our hope is sole-

ly in God, a Father who calls us uncompromisingly
to covenant love. Our hope is in Jesus, who demands simply, "Follow me!" Our hope is in the
Spirit who ever enlightens and challenges us, even
in the very midst of uncertainty, sin, misery, poverty, famine, confusion and change. Such a morality
is not easy: it calls for all we have.

With focus on the person, the new morality
stresses the central and radical importance of freedom and responsibility. It does so in a way that
makes *growth* in freedom the goal of our life, and
sees responsibility as embracing all life. We are
free; so *we* must be responsible. There is no substitute; there is no "out"; there are no magic formulas
or pat answers in which to escape. We are responsible for the direction of our life, for all our attitudes
and habits, for all our decisions and activity.

We are flesh-and-blood, body-soul persons, existing in time and space, very limited in freedom,
influenced by innumerable factors of heredity, environment, temperament, talent, education, culture and religion. Yet as persons we are graced by
God and called to sonship and union. We are
called, and we have the ability to respond and grow
in freedom and love.

The supreme unifying and normative principle
of the new morality is: *Be responsible!* Seek in
every situation to love your brothers as Jesus loves
you, to grow as a person-sinner-graced. Grow in
freedom, grow in doing good. Do the best you can,
prefer the greater good. You'll never quite know
you have done enough. The Gospel always demands more.

Some may feel that there is not enough concern about individual acts or sins. In maintaining that they can be evaluated only in terms of basic option, whole-life orientation, the new morality is simply pointing to the total motivation and meaning behind all individual acts, instead of considering them as isolated from the rest of life. As our Lord said, "If you bring your gift to the altar and there recall that your brother has anything against you, leave your gift at the altar, go first and be reconciled with your brother, and then come and offer your gift." In other words, the new morality says about every action: this action is not isolated; no matter what it looks like from the outside, it must be judged in the light of your basic relationship with God and man.

Again, the new morality seems to have too much "love" for some people, not enough hell and damnation, punishment and "strictness." Such a view is not only contrary to the Gospel, it is a distortion of the very meaning of morality and can only result in childishness and immaturity.

Nothing is "stricter" than real love. All the laws in the world, all the penalties men can devise, cannot make the demands that love makes and gladly answers. There is no punishment worse than knowing one has betrayed a loved one, been unfaithful to a commitment made in truth and love. Hell is simply the final, total failure to love.

It is probable, even inevitable, that human persons, who are sinners, will at times abuse freedom and express themselves in very harmful and unloving ways — all under the guise of love and freedom.

171

But the answer is not to play God and try to decide how and to what extent others should be "allowed" freedom, or should be told precisely in what way to "love." The answer lies in the conviction that Jesus is risen and is present and operative through the Spirit in the hearts of men, in the belief that most persons are basically good, sincere, and striving to grow.

The new morality seeks to reflect the Gospel: *faith, conversion, growth, freedom, love.* Traditionally morality, in its way, sought to do the same. We believe that the new morality reflects the Gospel more accurately and enables one to live the Gospel more consistently, wholeheartedly and fruitfully. That's what morality is all about. This is what makes the new morality "new" and provides its justification.

We don't know for sure. Time will tell. "By their fruits you will know them."